The Social Evolution of Humanity

Marx and Engels were right!

Bob McCubbin

The Social Evolution of Humanity:
Marx and Engels were right!

By Bob McCubbin

Copyright © 2019
ISBN: 9781698577968

Struggle for Socialism ★ La Lucha por Socialismo
Struggle-La-Lucha.org
Twitter: @StruggleLaLucha
Facebook.com/strugglelalucha
email: info@struggle-la-lucha.org

East Coast office
2011 N. Charles St., Baltimore, MD 21218
Phone: 443.221.3775

West Coast office
5278 W. Pico Blvd., Los Angeles, CA 90019
Phone: 323.306.6240

The art work on the cover was created by Don Reed in 1990 around the time of the first show of his paintings in downtown Brooklyn. Reed's brilliant art was the socially conscious expression of a Black gay artist exploring the glory and the pain of his community.

Reed and his partner Steve Schultz struggled to break new ground in being one of the first gay couples to adopt a child. After Reed and Shultz died in the AIDS epidemic their child was raised as a treasured member of their family.

The photo of Bob McCubbin on the back cover was taken at a protest during the height of the Gay Liberation movement.

The type used in this book is Minion Pro, Encode Sans and Open Sans.

The Social Evolution of Humanity:
Marx and Engels were right!

This study of the evolution of humanity focuses on human social/sexual relations and, in particular, the changing social status of women.

It offers a selection of scientific evidence that updates and augments the viewpoint expressed in Frederick Engels' masterful work, *Origin of the Family, Private Property and the State.*

– Bob McCubbin

Acknowledgements

Humanity presently exists in a world rent with division. The global ruling-class enemy benefits greatly from this atomization of society. As a communist, my personal energy and efforts are a modest addition to the collective energy, efforts and dedication of my comrade members of the Socialist Unity Party, a new Marxist-Leninist formation which has joined the ongoing global struggle for human liberation and socialism.

I want to acknowledge and thank each and every founding member of the SUP: Jefferson Azevedo, Miranda Bachman, Sharon Black, Greg Butterfield, David Card, Steven Ceci, Andrew Concon, Bill Dores, Reece Evans, Mary Lou Finley, Zola Fish, Roy Fleming, Brandon Harris, Rebecka Jackson, Berta Joubert-Ceci, Cody Kiridžija, Cheryl LaBash, Kermit Leibensperger, Steve Millies, Carl Muhammad, M. Matsemela-Ali Odom, John Thompson Parker, Lee Patterson, Andre Powell, Anne Pruden, Scott Scheffer, Lallan Schoenstein, Alec Summerfield, M. Tiahui, Lizz Toledo-Reid, Maggie Vascassenno, Gloria Verdieu, Renee Washington and Gary Wilson.

Very special thanks and heartfelt gratitude must be directed to Lallan Schoenstein and Gary Wilson, both of whom read the manuscript and offered valuable criticism. And to Lallan Schoenstein for her relentless encourage-ment of the author and her tireless hard work in applying her great artistic and technical skills so that this work could see the light of day. Much love to Lallan and Gary.

CONTENTS

Three lives worth emulating

This work is dedicated to Rosemary Neidenberg, who won me to communism; Dorothy Ballan, who mentored me on how to be a good communist; and Leslie Feinberg, who taught me that the challenge to patriarchal capitalism must include the struggle against gender-based oppression.

Rosemary Neidenberg

Rosemary Neidenberg (1921-) is a lifelong communist and founding member of Workers World Party, whose anger at imperialism remains undiminished and whose vision of a socialist future for humankind is uncompromised after her many decades of struggle with the goal of the establishment of workers' power here in the world center of capitalism.

Asking her forgiveness for the betrayal of the private communication that follows, the present author couldn't resist including in this dedication her recent email message concerning a work unknown to me, but obviously of significance and value to the present effort to deepen working-class consciousness and knowledge of our species' prehistory and history:

Rosemary Neidenberg on the left.

Neidenberg writes:

> Read the review [of *The Biggest Estate on Earth: How Aboriginal People Made Australia* by Bill Gammage]. It will make you boil with rage. Another example of how white Europeans found heaven and replaced it with hell. Reminds me of how the god-damned English imperialists destroyed the irrigation system in India.

She then pastes in a blurb of the book's contents:

> "This is an extraordinary book that details how Australian Aboriginal people cared for the land, or as Bill Gammage calls it, the *'Biggest Estate on Earth.'*
>
> "Gammage describes, with many examples, how Aboriginal people looked after the land. No corner was ignored, from deserts and rainforests to rocky outcrops, across the entire continent for at least 60,000 years until British colonisers began to destroy all this work after their arrival in 1788."

Rosemary Neidenberg! Live like her!

Photo: Minnie Bruce Pratt

Rosemary Neidenberg, Milt Niedenberg
and Leslie Feinberg in 2008

Dorothy Ballan

Dorothy Ballan (1918-1992) made enormous contributions to the struggle for human liberation over the course of her lifetime. From the brief bio in *Feminism and Marxism* — her 1971 materialist analysis of the role of women through history and, at the same time, a powerful polemic against the bourgeois view of the women's liberation movement of that period — we learn of her pioneering trade union work as a young factory worker.

She began as a volunteer organizer and then became a full-time organizer for the United Paper Workers Union, CIO, in New York City. Later, in Buffalo, she fought successfully for women in the electrical industry to work as diesetters, a job category previously denied to women. As a shop steward, she defended the rights of about 1,000 workers. Then, as an elected executive board member, she became one of the top four leaders of Local 1581 of the International Union of Electrical Workers, CIO-AFL.

Dorothy Ballan was a founding member of Workers World Party. Having survived the decade and more of McCarthyite repression undaunted and politically strong, she, her lifetime partner Sam Marcy, and a handful of like minded revolutionists, seized the opportunity to revive revolutionary Marxism in the United States. They quickly attracted angry, anti-racist, anti-war youth who made the party's youth group, Youth Against War and Fascism, "the cutting edge of the left," in the words of one progressive Black journalist of the time.

Ballan had multiple roles in the party. She led the party's political line on women and LGBTQ people. Her booklet,

Feminism and Marxism, found a receptive audience among the young militants of the time. Following the 1969 Stonewall Rebellion, she initiated an extensive series of party classes to raise party consciousness about and active support for what was termed, at the time, the Gay Liberation movement. Her analysis laid the groundwork for the party's theoretical understanding of this issue.

In collaboration with her life partner, she exercised great wisdom in the creation of party structures that would allow this combat party to, as Sam Marcy used to say, be able "to spin on a dime."

Finally, Dorothy Ballan had a special sensitivity to and understanding of the secret sufferings of the human heart, the inevitable interpersonal misunderstandings of even the most empathetic comrades. She spent countless hours at one-on-one meetings, helping comrades sort out personal matters. Dottie, I can still hear your slow but steady foot falls as you ascended the long flight of stairs at 46 West 21st Street, the party's longtime national headquarters, after another long day working for the boss.

Dorothy Ballan, a Bolshevik in thought and action!

Dorothy Ballan
and Sam Marcy

Leslie Feinberg

Leslie Feinberg (1949-2014)! What brief bio could possibly capture the incredibly rich life and remarkable contributions of this revolutionary communist and transgender leader?

Leslie and I both spent our early childhood years in the working-class community of North Buffalo, but she was almost a decade younger than me and we never crossed paths back then. In fact, we only met in the early 1970s when she moved to New York City, having first joined and spent time in the Buffalo branch of Workers World Party.

By the way, why do I use the pronouns "she" and "her" referring to Leslie? Leslie did experiment with gender pronoun innovations, but once confided to me that she thought there was educational value for onlookers in the apparent contradiction between her physical appearance and the verbal references to her using "she" and "her."

On page 16 of *Transgender Warriors*, one of her groundbreaking books, Leslie describes a chance encounter in the Buffalo Workers World office with branch organizer Ed Merrill:

"One night, he found me standing in the WWP literature room with tears in my eyes." What Leslie is describing here was her frustration, as a young transgender factory worker who, in her own words, barely made it through high school. She continues, "I had made it a policy not to read non-fiction books, because I feared I wasn't smart enough to understand the facts inside."

She goes on to describe how Ed then took on the task of guiding her with book suggestions and frequent one-on-one meetings: "I spent many exciting hours talking to Eddy about politics. Before he lent me each book, he'd talk to me about it. After I'd read it, we would sit and discuss the ideas."

A few decades later, Leslie had become an in-demand speaker on transgender issues, not just within the borders of the U.S., but worldwide. Her open identification as a communist, as a national leader of Workers World Party, seemed never to be an obstacle. She received a warm welcome everywhere she traveled to, and the love of her trans sisters, brothers and others.

Leslie stood before a crowd of thousands in New York City's Madison Square Garden theater and demanded freedom for longtime political prisoner Mumia Abu-Jamal. She worked tirelessly as a managing editor of the party's weekly newspaper. She found the time to write two widely praised novels and three theory laden works on gender diversity and the struggle for transgender liberation.

Finally, Leslie had a truly remarkable capacity for love. Read **Stone Butch Blues**.

Leslie Feinberg, ¡Siempre presente!

Photo: Rainbow Solidarity in defense of Cuba

Michael Callen, Leslie Feinberg and Bobbie Cambell at first national AIDS protest in October 1983.

A personal note and an Introduction

The present author opened the pages of the *New York Times* one day in late June of 1969 and the title of one short article on an inner page hit him smack in the face: "Homosexuals Riot in Greenwich Village." You had to have lived through the horribly repressive culture of the 1950s. You had to have felt the fear on a daily basis that your illegal and widely despised sexuality would be discovered to appreciate what those five words meant to this young political activist.

It took six more months of soul searching, of struggling to find the courage, but he did finally come out, but only after leaving his hometown of Buffalo, N.Y. He joined the San Francisco Gay Liberation Front shortly after he arrived in that city in January 1970. Then, after relocating to New York City a year and a half later, he came out to the whole New York City branch of Workers World Party on a fall day in 1971. He remembers a few seconds of total silence, and then, thunderous applause.

The party already had a history of sensitivity to and acceptance of gender diversity and homosexuality. But it wasn't articulated. There were no respectful formulations back then except the class conscious generalization that "we highly value all members of our class, especially the most oppressed." This was the position of the party's founders and it guided their attitudes and their behavior throughout their lives.

Sometime in the early 1970s, the present writer read Frederick Engels' ***Origin of the Family, Private Property and the State***. What an amazing book! Women had not always been oppressed! In fact, they had played important, even crucial roles in the advancement of our species over hundreds of thousands of years. Now he had a new reason to hate capitalism. It was the overthrow of early communal society's mother-right and the division of society into classes of

Bob and Minnie on a hike.

rich and poor, that had brought about the inferior status of women worldwide.

Comrade Dorothy Ballan saw the connection between the oppression of women and the oppression of LGBTQ2S folk. It only remained to fill in some of the details. That was done with the party's publication of *The Gay Question* (later retitled *The Roots of Lesbian and Gay Oppression*) in 1976. This work stands, as far as we have been able to determine, as the first Marxist effort on this issue.

Where that work fell short was on the issue of gender oppression. Comrade Leslie Feinberg fixed that with her germinal writings (See the entries for her published work in this book's "Bibliography").

In the present work, the focus will be on an effort to update Engels' *Origin* book with a multitude of supportive scientific findings and assessments that have appeared in print since the publication of that historic groundbreaker in 1884.

The present writer is neither an archaeologist nor an anthropologist nor a zoologist nor an ethnologist nor a historian. He has no special expertise in any of the sciences except for Marxism, the science of society. His academic background is in the field of linguistics, specifically applied linguistics. And while he is familiar with the literary technique of paraphrasing, he has preferred, in most cases seen in this work, to let the historians, scientists and theoreticians speak for themselves in their own words. Hopefully, he has shown good judgement in choosing which passages best represent each author's meaning. He sincerely apologizes for any unintended misrepresentations.

CHAPTER 1

Marriage –
two schools of thought lock horns

Although the issue of the legality of same-sex marriage appears to be settled, at least in the United States, with the June 2015 Supreme Court ruling, in the case of **Obergefell v. Hodges**, that this formal agreement between two people, regardless of their sex and/or gender, is protected by the U.S. Constitution, it is useful in hindsight to revisit the ideological opposition to this right as an example of the powerful reactionary forces that are always available, under the rule of capitalism, to hinder social progress.

Marriage: Everywhere and always the same?

"Marriage is a binding contract between one man and one woman for the establishment of an individual family." In years past, in response to the demand for marriage equality, people heard slight variations on this basic formulation over and over again, from numerous conservative politicians, religious leaders, radio and TV talk show hosts and garden-variety, right-wing bigots, as the struggle for same-sex marriage rights heated up in states across the U.S. and at the very heights of bourgeois political power in Washington, D.C.

Surprisingly, though, these quoted words come not from any contemporary "authority" on the subject, but from the mouth of a prominent 20th century anthropologist defending "traditional" marriage in a debate that took place many years ago.

Polish-born Bronislaw Malinowski is known as the founder of social anthropology. He was born in 1884, held academic posts in both Britain and the U.S. during the course of his career, and did anthropological fieldwork in many areas of the world, including Papua New Guinea and the Trobriand Islands. His writings are considered anthropological landmarks. He died in Mexico in 1942.

Robert Briffault, also of European origin, was born in 1876. His monumental, three-volume contribution to anthropology, *The Mothers*, was published in 1927. He died in 1948.

Marriage, Past and Present: A Debate Between Robert Briffault and Bronislaw Malinowski (Briffault 1956) provides a transcript of the 1931 BBC broadcasts where these two giants of anthropology locked horns.

Malinowski's position throughout the debate series was to repeatedly deny that there has ever been, throughout the whole history of human social evolution, any significant variation in the form by which societies organized their members for sexual and reproductive purposes:

> Through all the changes and vicissitudes of history and development, the family and marriage still remain the same twin institution; they still emerge as a stable group showing throughout the same characteristics: the group consisting of father and mother and their children, forming a joint household, co-operating economically, legally united by a contract and surrounded by religious sanctions which make the family into a moral unit. (80)

The foundation of marriage: romance or economic considerations?

Briffault countered that:

> If, following out the various forms of the institution of marriage, we work our way up from the Australian black [the Indigenous peoples that Briffault references as an example of pre-agricultural and pre-pastoral societies], through the various stages in the evolution of culture, glancing at the matrimonial arrangements of African chiefs [tribal societies], or Chinese mandarins [slavery/feudalism], up to those of a French peasant or of an English duke [feudalism], we shall find in every quarter of the globe and in every age that the transaction rests chiefly, and in most instances exclusively, upon economic considerations. (55-56)

Malinowski, however, insists that the basis of all marriage is romantic love:

> There is nothing more important to realise with regard to the institution of marriage than that it is everywhere based on love and affection. (68)

Briffault's rejoinder rests on his prodigious knowledge of pre-agricultural and pre-pastoral societies.

> Our reports and observations about savages [this is the unfortunate word that anthropologists used for many years to describe societies whose food sources were based on hunting animals and foraging for plants] are very emphatic and uniform as to the absence of romantic love amongst them. (56)

Briffault explains this by contrasting the social conditions of communal, band-based and clan-based societies with those of more technologically developed societies riven by class divisions:

> Among savages, who are every bit as affectionate as we are, affection is not concentrated on the man-woman relation; it is diffused in the comradeship of the clan. The savage, as a general rule, is quite kind and tender to his women. But no more so to his wife than to his mother or sisters or his brothers or children of the clan. The most definite and unanimous testimonies which we have of affection between man and woman among savages refer to the devotion between very old married couples. In other words, love among savages is the result, rather than the cause of marriage. (57)

Malinowski is adamant in this debate that another foundation of what he terms "the individual family" is the need to "legitimize" the children. Briffault responds:

> Where women remain after marriage in their own home and among their people, and the husband joins them there, the children belong to their mother's clan. A child is not the heir to his father's property or to his name, he derives both from his mother and from his relatives. One consequence of that organisation and that form of marriage, which we call matrilocal, is that there are no illegitimate children. (58)

Later on he continues:

> A legal contract is required to make a child legitimate only where he must inherit his father's name and property. (59)

Providing a historical context as communal societies began to give way to societies with class divisions, Briffault notes:

> Among many people, such as the Samoans, there are very elaborate marriage contracts and ceremonies, but only in the case of chiefs and owners of important property. The common and poor people, although they may bring up large families, are not said to marry, but to live at their pleasure in concubinage [cohabitation without a legal marriage]. (59)

The counterrevolution in anthropology

In *Feminism and Marxism*, an important polemic in booklet form addressed to the women's liberation movement of the 1970s, Workers World Party founder and leader Dorothy Ballan comments on the ideological struggle between the original, historical materialist approach to anthropology and the bourgeois school that has come to dominate this social science:

> What is involved here is whether to accept the revolutionary teachings of the historical materialist school of thought as expounded by Engels (and in part based on the researches of Lewis H. Morgan) or whether to take the bourgeois anti-evolutionist position, which has dominated anthropology in this country for many decades. The latter aims as one of its principal objectives to discredit, disqualify and destroy the monumental contributions of Morgan and Engels. (40)

The anti-evolutionary school of anthropology represented by Malinowski and other well-known anthropologists of the 20th century has been seriously undermined by the work of contemporary anthropologists, many of whom hold the groundbreaking formulations of Lewis Henry Morgan and Frederick Engels in high regard. In forthcoming chapters, we'll attempt to summarize the important insights these two historic figures contributed to the origins and development of human social, sexual, productive and reproductive relations.

CHAPTER 2

The challenge of uncovering hominin/human prehistory

Chapter 1 focused on Bronislaw Malinowski's views on the institution of marriage as an example of the counterrevolution in anthropology that arose in response to the work of Lewis Henry Morgan and Frederick Engels, whose findings projected an evolutionary history of human development. In this chapter, we'll raise some preliminary considerations toward an objective, scientific investigation of human prehistory. In following chapters, we'll take up the discoveries of Morgan and Engels in some detail.

In the present effort, we are guided by the profound groundwork provided in Frederick Engels' *Origin of the Family, Private Property and the State* and the deft summarization and contemporary application of his work in Dorothy Ballan's booklet, *Feminism and Marxism*. There is, of course, no real substitute for a serious, focused reading of these two essential works in their entirety.

In later chapters of the present effort, we will review some of the more recent explorations of human history and prehistory, unavailable to either Engels or Ballan. But, first, we should examine some of the insights provided by the groundbreakers.

A scientific approach to human prehistory

In her "Introduction" to the International Publishers edition of Engels' *Origin* (1972), Marxist anthropologist Eleanor Leacock notes:

> Where materials are available for ethnohistorical research into a given primitive culture, they reveal fundamental changes of the type that have been taking place independently in various parts of the world or have been developing rapidly during the recent centuries of colonial rule: the breaking down of the corporate kin group into individual families and the individualization of property rights, the downgrading of women's status, the strengthening of rank, and the usurpation of powers by chiefs — in short, the basis for class society.
>
> Nonetheless, areas where warfare and trade, often in slaves as well as goods, have been causing vast upheavals for up to four or five centuries of European influence and domination are still commonly treated as if reconstructed 19th century social forms represent "untouched" institutions. (58-59)

We will avoid the use of the word "primitive" to characterize prehistoric societies and, similarly, use of the word "civilized" to describe the class-divided societies that have followed, since it needs to be emphasized more and more, as contemporary foraging and hunting groups succumb to the genocidal impact of the world's imperialist powers, how remarkably "civilized" these peoples were in their interpersonal relations and how scientific in their use of natural resources in their efforts at survival. However, we can totally agree with Leacock on the need to apply a very critical eye to ethnographic reports.

The historical materialist approach

Karl Marx was fascinated by the ethnographic material he found in Lewis Henry Morgan's book, *Ancient Society*, but Marx died before he was able to accomplish the task of interpreting it. Engels, Marx's lifelong collaborator, took up the task, resulting in *Origin* and an uncompleted work titled *The Part Played by Labor in the Transition from Ape to Man.*

While Marx and Engels were thoroughly cognizant of the difficulties alluded to by Leacock a century later, they had a powerful theoretical tool for use in evaluating Morgan's ethnographic material. Known as historical materialism, their method broke with the then prevailing approach of European philosophers who, in their various interpretations of the world, assumed the priority of ideas over matter.

Marx's approach emphasized human sociality and production of the wherewithal for the sustenance of life as fundamental to humanity's reality and evolution. Also fundamental to Marx's approach was the inextricable link between material reality and dialectical change. (A very clear and succinct explanation of dialectical materialism is given by Russian revolutionary leader, Leon Trotsky, in his book, *In Defense of Marxism.*)

Just as the material reality of revolutionary French workers setting up a workers' government in 1871 — the Paris Commune — allowed Marx and Engels to concretize their prediction of workers' political power and of a workers' government that could lay the groundwork for a socialist/communist future, so too, the patterns of social life and kinship that Morgan reported on from his personal contact with the tribes of the Iroquois Confederacy, other Native American groups, and reports he received on hunting and gathering groups across the globe, offered a material basis for Engels to project the evolution of humanity from communal beginnings, through the various stages of class society, to a communist future — really to a final reclaiming of Homo sapiens' original communal humanity, but with the benefits that have accrued from continuing technological advances in our relations with the rest of the material world.

Chapter 3 will examine the findings of Lewis Henry Morgan, the founder of modern anthropology, regarding the role of women in early human societies. As we shall see, understanding the social position of women in foraging and hunting societies is crucial to understanding the forms of "marriage" that existed in that long period of human prehistory.

Pre-class communalists

The 550 pages of Lewis Henry Morgan's *Ancient Society* reveal how Morgan was able to draw on a huge amount of then existing ethnographic information on clan-based societies all over the world.

This said, the reader will note that the section on pairing marriages references, specifically, North American Indigenous peoples. Morgan's interest in Indigenous societies was seeded, stimulated and informed by his long friendship with Ely S. Parker, whom Elisabeth Tooker, in her "Forward" to *Ancient Society*, describes as "a young Tonawanda Seneca of remarkable gifts." It was Parker, Tooker tells us, who shared with Morgan detailed knowledge of Iroquois (Haudenosaunee) customs and culture. (xix)

Morgan gave special recognition to his use of the ethnographic material provided in Johann Jakob Bachofen's *Das Mutterrecht (Mother Right)* of 1861:

> In a work of vast research, Bachofen has collected
> and discussed the evidence of female authority (mother-
> right) and of female rule (gyneocracy) among the Lycians,
> Cretans, Athenians, Lemnians, Egyptians, Orchomenians,
> Loerians, Lesbians, Mantineans, and among eastern Asiatic
> nations. (349)

He also credits the reports of numerous other observers of pre-class and early class, Indigenous societies in North America, Australia and elsewhere.

Terminological considerations

The various labels that have been used in discussing the different stages of early human social groups can be confusing and, occasionally, off-putting. The earliest groupings of our ancestors, perhaps covering both humans and pre-human species and believed to be small in number and migratory, are usually referred to as "bands," although the word "hordes" is also encountered.

We find the whole earliest period of human evolution referred to as "savagery" in many older texts and the following period, composed of clans and tribal societies, as "barbarism." Morgan used the word "gens" (plural form "gentes" and adjective form "gentile") to describe the basic organizational unit of the Iroquois (the Haudenosaunee) peoples of New York state, whom he had extensive personal knowledge of, but also more generally for this form of social organization. Such social groupings are, in contemporary texts, referred to as "clans" and consist of kin who, in theory at least, are all descended from a common female ancestor.

Clans are distinguished from "tribes," which are associations of clans and are groupings where we find the beginnings of male political and economic leadership roles in the process of historical social evolution toward what is referred to as "civili-

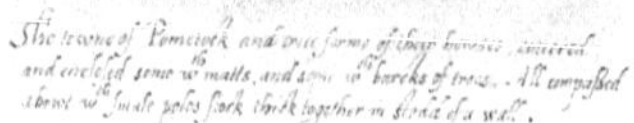

zation," another frequently used word that should be pronounced with tongue in cheek. What is meant is human societies that have arrived at a certain level of technological development, but which are lacking communality, divided as they are into classes of rich and poor.

The matrilineal clan

Morgan's research on matrilineal clans was almost global in its extent. Thus, the generalizations he formulated had a firm basis in reality.

Morgan describes a basic aspect of gentile society:

> The council was the great feature of ancient society. ...
> The simplest and lowest form of the council was that
> of the gens. It was a democratic assembly because
> every adult male and female member had a voice upon
> all questions brought before it. It elected and deposed its
> sachem and chiefs. ...
>
> All the members of an Iroquois gens were personally
> free, and they were bound to defend each other's freedom;
> they were equal in privileges and in personal rights, the
> sachem and chiefs claiming no superiority; and they were a
> brotherhood bound together by the ties of kin. Liberty,
> equality, and fraternity, though never formulated, were
> cardinal principles of the gens. (84-85)

The matrilineal character of the early gentes, worldwide, is a theme to which Morgan returns repeatedly in *Ancient Society*:

> A gens in the archaic period consisted of a supposed
> female ancestor and her children, together with the
> children of her daughters, and of her female descendants
> through females in perpetuity. The children of her sons,
> and of her male descendants, through males, were
> excluded. (343-344)

Iroquois longhouse

Photo: Saint Regis Mohawk Tribe

Further ramifications of this form of social organization included the fact that the sons of male leaders could not inherit their father's status or position. Neither could sons inherit the property of their father ("property," which invariably would have been modest in value and personal in character, such as tools, ritual gear, weapons, etc.).

The 'pairing' marriage and its antecedent

Among the Indigenous peoples of North America, Morgan found what he termed "pairing families." He considered this form to have developed from an earlier one:

> The large groups in the marriage relation, which must have existed in the previous period [and] disappeared; and, in their place were married pairs, forming clearly marked, though but partially individualized families. … Several of [these families] were usually found in one house, forming a communal household, in which the principle of communism in living was practiced. The fact of the conjunction of several such families in a common household is of itself an admission that the family was too feeble an organization to face alone the hardships of life. (453)

Specifically, with regard to marriage among these peoples, Morgan writes:

Interior of Iroquois longhouse

But the marriage institution was as peculiar as the family. Men did not seek wives as they are sought in civilized society, from affection, for the passion of love … was unknown among them. Marriage, therefore, was not founded upon sentiment but upon convenience and necessity.

It was left to the mothers, in effect, to arrange the marriage of their children, and they were negotiated generally without the knowledge of the parties to be married, and without asking their previous consent. It sometimes happened that entire strangers were thus brought into the marriage relation. At the proper time they were notified when the simple nuptial ceremony would be performed.

Such were the usages of the Iroquois and many other Indian tribes. Acquiescence in these maternal contracts was a duty which the parties seldom refused. … The relation … continued during the pleasure of the parties, and no longer. It is for this reason that it is properly distinguished as the pairing family. The husband could put away his wife at pleasure and take another without offence, and the woman enjoyed the equal right of leaving her husband and accepting another. (454)

In a footnote on page 455, Morgan quotes a missionary who spent many years among the Senecas:

As to their family system, when occupying the old long-houses, it is probable that some one clan predominated, the women taking in husbands, however, from the other clans; and sometimes, for a novelty, some of their sons bringing in their young wives until they felt brave enough to leave their mothers. Usually, the female portion ruled the house, and were doubtless clannish enough about it.

The stores were in common; but woe to the luckless husband or lover who was too shiftless to do his share of the providing. No matter how many children, or whatever goods he might have in the house, he might at any time be ordered to pick up his blanket and budge; and after such orders it would not be healthful for him to attempt to disobey. The house would be too hot for him; and, unless saved by the intercession of some aunt or grandmother, he must retreat to his own clan; or, as was often done, go and start a new matrimonial alliance in some other.

The women were the great power among the clans, as everywhere else. They did not hesitate, when occasion required, "to knock off the horns," as it was technically called, from the head of a chief, and send him back to the ranks of the warriors. The original nomination of the chiefs also always rested with them.

The reference in the first sentence of this quotation to the "taking in [of] husbands … from the other clans" alludes to two important features of the pairing family: the exogamous character of clan marriage (always marrying outside one's own clan) and matrilocality (the husband leaving his clan to join the wife's clan).

More on marriage in the Iroquois Confederacy

An earlier work by Morgan, *League of the Iroquois*, covers all aspects of traditional Haudenosaunee society and includes a detailed description of marriage customs within the Iroquois Confederacy.

For this work, Morgan relied heavily on the assistance of his much esteemed friend, Seneca Native Ely S. Parker. In the "Introduction" to the 1996 reprint of the 1851 original edition, William N. Fenton, himself a respected student of Haudenosaunee history and culture, describes Parker as:

> [O]ne of those rare individuals ... at home in both cultures. As interpreter he had access to sources on tribal government, his family was a natural entrée for Morgan into Seneca society. ...
>
> Parker as a newly elected honorary member came to Aurora [a town in the Finger Lakes region of New York state where Morgan's Grand Order of the Iroquois group met] to lecture the Grand Order on the harsh realities of Indian life. (X)

But, as an Indigenous person, Parker could not escape the pervasive racism of U.S. society. Although his remarkable erudition gained him fame and prompted an invitation to Washington, D.C., to meet the U.S. president:

> [Parker] felt the curious gaze of other tourists and sensed what it was to be a slave. ... He attended church, and was directed to sit in the gallery with the Negros. The usher did not perceive a rising civil engineer, the future aide-de-camp of General U.S. Grant, or the sometime Commissioner of Indian Affairs. (XI)

Morgan's characterization of the League's governance includes the following summary sentence in *League of the Iroquois*:

> Running through their whole system of administration, was a public sentiment, which gave its own tendency to affairs, and illustrated to a remarkable degree, that the government rested upon the popular will, and not upon the arbitrary sway of chiefs. (75-76)

Nevertheless, he repeatedly uses the term "oligarchy" in

referring to the Council of the League (perhaps because council membership depended only in part on the democratic election of leaders). But the deferential responsiveness of the council members to popular opinion, the public character of council meetings (with mass attendance) and the firm council guideline that demanded universal consensus before any action could be taken bespeak a measure of democracy that the citizens of present-day Western "democracies" can only marvel at.

The unifying function of the marriage system

Morgan notes that the form of organization under which the Council of the League functioned was duplicated in the governing body of each of the five (and later a sixth) member tribes [the Mohawks, Oneidas, Onondagas, Cayugas and Senecas, and later the Tuscaroras], tribes also known collectively as "the People of the Long House."

What united these tribes even more firmly than their League and tribal councils was, according to Morgan, their marriage system:

> With the ties of kindred as its principle of union, the whole [Confederacy] was interwoven into one great family, composed of tribes in its first subdivision … and the tribes themselves, in their subdivisions, composed of parts of many households. Without these close inter-relations, resting, as many do, upon the strong impulses of nature, a mere alliance between the Iroquois nations would have been feeble and transitory. (82)

Morgan describes both an earlier marriage pattern and the pattern in existence at the time of his writing and concludes:

> Under the original as well as modern regulation, the husband and wife were of different tribes. The children always followed the tribe of the mother. (83)

CHAPTER 4

Marx and Engels on Morgan's analysis

As noted previously, Karl Marx and Frederick Engels found Morgan's analysis of pre-class and early class society of great value. In the "Preface to the First Edition" of *Origin,* Engels writes:

> Karl Marx had made it one of his future tasks to present the results of Morgan's researches in the light of the conclusions of his own — within certain limits, I may say our — materialistic examination of history, and thus to make clear their full significance. (71)

Morgan's findings were based not on religious dogma or philosophical meanderings, but rather on a consistently objective approach, a scientific approach, to the reality of existing clan and tribal societies.

Engels offered a profound tribute to Morgan:

> This rediscovery of the primitive matriarchal gens as the earlier stage of the patriarchal gens of civilized peoples has the same importance for anthropology as Darwin's theory of evolution has for biology and Marx's theory of surplus value for political economy. (83)

'The part played by labor'

What Engels was able to add in *Origin* to Morgan's conclusions was a political perspective based on how human technological innovations, like the development of plant cultivation and the domestication of animals, affected the productivity of human labor. He explained how this increasing productivity affected human social relations, specifically the role and position of women, and social development, resulting ultimately in the division of society into antagonistic social classes of rich and poor based on private property and the alienation of people from the products of their labor.

> Labor is the source of all wealth, the political economists assert. It is this, next to nature, which supplies it with the material that it converts into wealth. But it is even infinitely more than this. It is the prime basic condition for all human existence, and this to such an extent that, in a sense, we have to say that labor created man himself. (7)

These intriguing words grace the beginning of Engels' unfinished essay, *The Part Played by Labor in the Transition from Ape to Man.* They also serve as an introduction to Engels' comments in **Origin** on the economic conditions of early humanity:

> At all earlier stages of society, production was essentially collective, just as consumption proceeded by direct distribution of the products within larger or smaller communistic communities. This collective production was very limited; but inherent in it was the producers' control over their process of production and their product. They knew what became of their product: they consumed it; it did not leave their hands. And so long as production remains on this basis, it cannot grow above the heads of the producers nor raise up incorporeal alien powers against them, as in civilization is always and inevitably the case. (233)

This distinction between production for use and, by implication, commodity production for private profit is crucial to an understanding of what it was that transformed the matrilineal societies that Morgan studied into the patriarchal societies that enslaved women and fundamentally altered marriage relations. Production for private profit is based on private ownership of the means of production and the alienation of the worker from the product of her or his or their labor.

The importance of women in production

Engels notes that the first division of labor was between men and women, specifically with regard to reproduction, "the propagation of children." But this was a benign division. A number of contemporary anthropologists argue that one of the things that distinguished our species and strengthened our survival potential was the willingness of men to cooperate in the care of children, at the very least by sharing meat.

Anthropologist Eleanor Leacock witnessed much more than meat sharing during her time spent with the Montagnais-Naskapi of the Labrador Peninsula:

> One of many incidents I observed must suffice to indicate what can lie behind the stereotyped ascription in monographic accounts of such people: the men hunt; the women gather berries and care for the children. For the greater part of one day a man sat patiently, lovingly crooning over his sickly and fretful infant of but a few weeks old. His wife was busy. Though worried for the baby's health, he appeared in no way inept or harassed by his responsibility, nor did he call on

Ihalmiut people care for the children.

another woman around the camp for help. His unself-conscious assurance and patience set him quite apart from latter-day readers of Dr. Spock [whose "baby book" guided mid 20th century parents in the U.S. through the travails of child raising]. This was his task while his wife tanned a caribou skin, a skilled and arduous job that demanded her complete attention. The men knew how to cook and tend the babies when called upon to do so, but did not really know how to tan leather. (Engels 1972: 39)

Both men and women contributed to the sustenance of the communal group and enjoyed equal social status. Anthropologist Richard Lee, in his paper titled, "What Hunters Do for a Living" (In Lee and DeVore 1968) concludes:

Since a 30 to 40 percent input of meat is such a consistent target for modern hunters [in foraging and hunting groups] in a variety of habitats, is it not reasonable to postulate a similar percentage for prehistoric hunters? (43)

In other words, the labor of women as foragers was crucial (although men also foraged). Women's foraging activities would have contributed the other 60 percent to 70 percent of the food supply. And this fact in no way diminishes women's role in hunting, both of small animals and in group roundup activities, and in scavenging, which some anthropologists think preceded hunting among early humans. Contemporary anthropologists also speculate that one of the first "tools" invented by women, along with the digging stick, was the baby sling, greatly increasing the mobility and productivity of mothers.

Primordial promiscuity

Engels was impressed by Morgan's ability to extrapolate the forms of sexual and kinship relations in the remote past based on the more complex forms existing in the gathering and hunting societies he was familiar with in the 19th century:

> The study of primitive history … reveals conditions where the men live in polygamy [multiple wives] and their wives in polyandry [multiple husbands] at the same time, and their common children are therefore considered common to them all — and these conditions in their turn undergo a long series of changes before they finally end in monogamy. The trend of these changes is to narrow more and more the circle of people comprised within the common bond of marriage, which was originally very wide, until at last it includes only the single pair, the dominant form of marriage today.
>
> Reconstructing thus the past history of the family, Morgan, in agreement with most of his colleagues, arrives at a primitive stage when unrestricted sexual freedom prevailed within the tribe, every woman belonging equally to every man and every man to every woman. Since the 18th century there had been talk of such a primitive state, but only in general phrases. Bachofen — and this is one of his great merits — was the first to take the existence of such a state seriously and to search for its traces in historical and religious survivals. Today, we know that the traces he found do not lead back to a social stage of promiscuous sexual intercourse, but to a much later form — namely, group marriage. The primitive social stage of promiscuity, if it ever existed, belongs to such a remote epoch that we can hardly expect to prove its existence directly by discovering its social fossils among backward savages. Bachofen's merit consists in having brought this question to the forefront for examination. (Engels 1972: 96-97)

We'll continue the discussion of primordial promiscuity among early humans in Chapter 7. And we'll return to Engels' **Origin** further along when we consider the changes wrought in the institutions of marriage and kinship by the victory of patriarchy over the matrilineal clans.

In the next chapter, however, we'll review contemporary studies of chimpanzees and bonobos (also referred to as pygmy chimpanzees) in their natural settings and in zoos. These scientific reports, which were lacking when Bachofen, Morgan and Engels were puzzling over the theoretical possibility of a remote past of "promiscuous sexual intercourse," offer the "traces" that we now might extrapolate into the distant past as possibly indicative of early hominin homosexual and heterosexual behavior.

CHAPTER 5

Promiscuous primates

Was Bronislaw Malinowski's conception of "a primeval and unchanging one-man, one-woman" marriage actually realized 5, 6, 7 or 8 million years ago, when our hominin ancestors parted company with their great ape cousins?

We don't think so. Our nearest relatives in the present day, our fellow great apes, show no such organizational form for purposes of sexual release, reproduction or otherwise.

While it's impossible to know for sure, we don't think the great apes' ancestors lived that way either, those millions of years ago when the hominin lineage split off:

> Genetic data tell us that the last common ancestor of humans, gorillas, and chimpanzees lived between 9 and 8 mya [million years ago] and the last common ancestor of humans and chimpanzees lived about 7 to 5 mya. (Boyd and Silk 2012: 216)

It's reasonable to speculate that, as with the many demonstrable anatomical similarities, early hominins would likely have had behavioral similarities to their primate relatives.

Jon Cohen's detailed report on his investigation of the ongoing scientific research in the field of primatology, *Almost Chimpanzee*, ends on a personal and provocative note:

> It was early afternoon, and I was sitting against a tree and resting from a long morning of chimping [observing and recording chimpanzee behavior in a natural setting] while

more than a dozen chimpanzees scattered about me in a midday siesta, reclining with one hand behind the head, picking through one another's hair, playing with their babies, quietly digesting food and thoughts from a busy morning . It was as though I had stumbled into a group of ancient humans. It was as though I was almost a chimpanzee myself. (314-315)

Mating habits among our genetic relatives

There's no evidence of "traditional marriage" among primates, except among gibbons, a distant cousin of ours.

But there's intriguing, detailed information on the mating habits of our two closest genetic relatives. The chimpanzees and the bonobos live disparate social/sexual lives. The details of their mating habits are in almost diametrical opposition.

While both species are promiscuous, both pre-eminent primatologist Frans de Waal (2005) and Richard Wrangham and Dale Peterson, the authors of **Demonic Males**, comment at length on the violence sometimes accompanying male chimpanzee approaches to females in estrus — periods of sexual receptivity. An interested male's violence may include fights with other interested males and/ or coercion, including kicking, slapping and slamming an unwilling female:

> Male attacks on females, so consistent and regular an aspect of chimpanzee life, might best be described by the term "battering." (Wrangham and Peterson 1996: 145)

De Waal notes similar behavior but is somewhat more cautious about generalizing. Reporting on observations made in the Kibale Forest in Uganda, he writes:

> The copycat spreading of this ugly habit [the battering
> of females] shows the extent to which apes are socially
> influenced. They often follow the example of others. We
> should be careful not to jump to conclusions about the
> "naturalness" of such behavior. Chimpanzee males are not
> programmed to beat females. (122)

To be cautious about overgeneralizing in any context is good advice, but on this issue it's important to note what Jane Goodall, the first primatologist to make in-the-wild observations of chimpanzees, wrote when describing male coercive behavior in Tanzania's Gombe National Park:

> Almost always … an adult male can coerce an unwilling
> female into copulating with him. (1986: 481)

Among bonobos, the women rule

Whatever the severity or extent of misogyny in chimpanzee groups, the contrast with male-female relations in bonobo groups could not be more dramatic. Contrasting with the dominant, or alpha males in chimp society, groups of females are the dominant social force in bonobo society. Wrangham and Peterson tell us:

> [Bonobos] are fascinating especially because of their
> remarkable females, who are in several ways more human-
> like than female chimpanzees. Bonobos present an extra-
> ordinary counterpoint to chimpanzees. … They have
> evolved ways to reduce violence that permeate their entire
> society. (26)

De Waal cites the observation of Japanese bonobo expert Takayoshi Kano that "food is exactly what female dominance is all about." De Waal notes:

> The collective rule of female bonobos is well-known at
> zoos, and fieldworkers must have begun to suspect the

same years before. But no one wanted to be the first to make such an outrageous claim, given how much male dominance is taken for granted in human evolution. Until 1992, that is, when scientists presented findings that left little doubt about bonobo girl power. One report looked at food competition in zoos, documenting how a male chimp living with two females will claim everything for himself, whereas a bonobo male under the same circumstances may not even be able to get near the food. He can make as many charging displays as he wants, but the females ignore the commotion and divide the food among themselves.

In the wild, an alpha female bonobo will stride into a clearing dragging a branch behind her, making a display that is avoided and watched by all others. It's not unusual for female bonobos to chase off the males, laying claim to the large fruits they divide among themselves. (66-67)

With regard to the lack of physical violence, male bonobos clearly benefit from the dominance of the females, writes de Waal:

Bonobo societies include equal numbers of males and females, whereas chimp societies often include twice as many females as males. Since both species have a one-to-one sex ratio at birth, and since there are no roaming males outside the community, chimp males must suffer extraordinary mortality. This is hardly surprising, given the intercommunity warfare of this species as well as the injuries and stress associated with continuous power struggles. The upshot is that male bonobos lead longer, healthier lives than their [violence-prone] counterparts. (68-69)

'Doing it' bonobo style

While male violence, including rape, in pursuit of sexual intercourse is common among chimpanzees and other apes, bonobo sex, while frequent, energetic and imaginative, is decidedly peaceful.

Jon Cohen's description is graphic:

> I live about thirty miles from the San Diego zoo, which hosts one of the few communities of captive bonobos anywhere in the world. I visit the bonobo exhibit frequently, and more often than not, I see males humping males, males and females engaging in "missionary position" coitus, or two females genito-genital rubbing their crotches. (254)

De Waal comments:

> The French kiss is the bonobo's most recognizable, human-like erotic act. Whenever I show an undergraduate class a film of my bonobos, the students get very quiet. … Invariably the deepest impression is made by a video clip of two juvenile males tongue-kissing. (90)

Criticized for overemphasizing "unconventional" sexual behavior, de Waal's rejoinder was short and to the point:

> When bonobos contact each other with their genitals
> (and squeal and show other signs of apparent orgasm),
> any sex therapist will tell you that they are "doing it."
> (Cohen 2010: 257)

It is, of course, a huge, imponderable leap from the social/sexual behavior of contemporary primate relatives of ours to the ancestors of these primates 6 million years ago, and then a further speculative leap to draw a comparison of their presumed social/sexual behavior with that of our own hominin ancestors at that remote stage of our evolution, whether we take for our chosen model typical bonobo or typical chimp behavior. Cohen writes:

Bonobos and chimpanzees, after all, are equidistant to humans on the evolutionary tree. So an alpha male chimp that dominates the females in a group is just as related to us as the bisexual bonobo female who dominates males in hers. (254)

What we can conclude with certainty is: There's no sign of "traditional marriage" among our closest relatives. Their sexual lives are characterized by promiscuity.

Photo: wcdumonts/Flickr

Bonobos

CHAPTER 6

Hominin origins and evolution

We turn now to paleoarchaeological speculation on the origins and early evolution of our species. In this section, we have relied on a few recent publications, the motive being that archaeological and primatological investigations, using ever more sophisticated technologies, have been able to produce ever more precise datings and ever more evidence-backed scenarios of and hypotheses regarding primate life and human prehistory. We'll also see, however, that signs of the anthropological counterrevolution discussed in Chapter 1 remain.

The datings for the initial appearance of "hominins" are clearly rough estimates but also a good reminder of the difficulty in pinpointing events over the incredibly long length of time our evolution has unfolded. (Here we should note that while in many of the works we consulted, the word "hominin" is used to refer to all the species of the family Hominidae, including all species in the genera Australopithecus and Homo, our use of it will be limited to references to the species predating the appearance of our species, Homo sapiens.)

Colin Renfrew, in his *Prehistory: The Making of the Human Mind*, estimates that the hominin lineage began between 8 and 6 million years ago. (48) Chris Scarre, editor of *The Human Past*, puts the date of emergence of bipedal hominins in Africa at 6 million years ago. (47)

As with the emergence of the first hominins, the important developments that eventually led to modern humans (Homo sapiens) can be only roughly dated. Before the beginnings of hominin brain expansion (approximately 2.5 million years ago) or even before the first use of fire (estimated at somewhere between 1.5 million and 700,000 years ago), it's highly likely that hominin life mirrored closely some of the patterns of life of the great ape relatives.

Communal hominins

What anthropologists and archaeologists have offered concerning the living patterns of ancient hominins are hypotheses — Chris Knight, a Marxist anthropologist, calls them "stories" or "myths" — based in part on examination of the few uncovered hominin bones and teeth that have survived the thousands of millennia; pieces of flint and other stones that appear to have been worked by hominins; climatic and botanical residue in ancient soils that provides evidence of climate changes that, in turn, might have impacted hominin life; and very sophisticated, radiometric techniques for dating these ancient materials.

The living patterns and beliefs of foraging and hunting groups still in existence during the most recent millennia — as described by observers as far back in time as the ancient Greek historian Herodotus (c. 484 B.C. — c. 425 B.C.) up to present-day archeologists and anthropologists — are also used to try to reconstruct the long process of hominin and human evolution.

The most commonly told story is that originally tree-dwelling, fruit-eating primates spent more and more time on the ground as the rainforests of East Africa slowly disappeared some 5 or so million years ago. The gradual disappearance of their former arboreal habitats forced dramatic adaptations, including bipedalism (standing and walking upright), plant foraging, scavenging and/or hunting animals, and a new emphasis on communalism and interpersonal communication.

Once out of the trees, group survival, it is said, necessitated cooperation, food sharing and organizing defense against predatory animals. An auspicious physiological change, the evolution of larger brains, may have been prompted by the challenges of this new physical environment, dramatic climate changes and the accompanying intensified sociality, which itself would have required a greater emphasis on interpersonal and social communication.

But our increasingly large brains created problems for the fetus' intrauterine development. Brains are also metabolically "expensive," their increasing size heightening the need for high-energy nutrition.

Successful births had to come sooner, while the neonate's head was still small enough to pass through the narrower pelvis produced by bipedalism. The result was the birth of totally helpless infants, unlike the babies of our primate ancestors. Prolonged postnatal care was required for their survival, but it also offered new, lengthier opportunities for the transmission of culture.

The control of fire and the development of language were further important advances that occurred at some point or span of time over this vast period of prehistory.

Scientists debate the timing, significance and details of these and other changes as the various hominin species evolved. But the central role of females as the producers of new life, as technological innovators, inventors of language and organizing agents of social life, is acknowledged by most.

The pivotal role of mothers to hominin society would of itself have bestowed great authority on females. But, in addition, the foraging skills of women were undoubtedly crucial to the band's continuing existence. Whether scavenging, fishing or hunting provided meat for the band, foraging for plant food would have been the more reliable source of nutrition in most situations and under most conditions. Small, usually nomadic hominin groups based on matrilineality would be the inevitable result.

So originally, in the remote past were tree-dwelling primates. Then came hunting, fishing and foraging bands of hominins. These hominins evolved, most likely, with gradual anatomical and behavioral changes based on natural selection and occasionally with dramatic, qualitative leaps. Eventually, several hundred thousand years ago, Homo sapiens — modern humans — appeared.

Debate is fierce in professional circles concerning when and how language and other nonmaterial or nondurable manifestations of human culture first appeared. In the most recent tens of thousands of years, though, clear traces of these foraging, fishing and hunting groups, along with artifacts left by technically and culturally advanced modern humans engaged in early pastoralist and horticultural activities, and in art, are more clearly apparent in the archeological record.

Persistence of the 'Malinowski' counterrevolution

Did "traditional marriage" appear at some point in the matrilineal hominin bands that had their origin and lived out their many generations in Africa? Or among the ones who, beginning more than 1 million years ago, began spreading out from Africa into Eurasia in several waves?

Many contemporary writers on the subject describe the hominin species' and the Homo sapiens' foraging and hunting bands that followed as composed of monogamous heterosexual pairs and their children. These writers accept as good science the view of monogamous pairing marriage as an eternal verity, more or less as articulated by Bronislaw Malinowski and other 20th century anthropologists of his ilk.

In Chapter 3 of *The Human Past*, paleoanthropologist Richard Klein writes that during the time span between 1.8 million and 600,000 to 500,000 years ago, hominin brain volume was increasing rapidly:

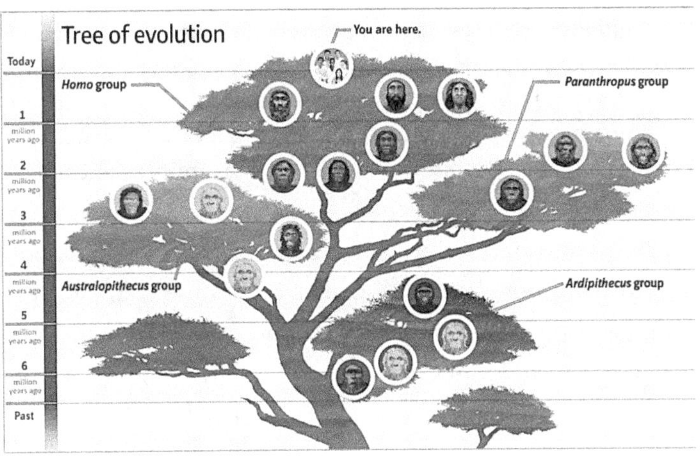

To an average firmly within the modern range. …
[And] the sexes did not exhibit any major dimorphism,
differing no more in size than they do in living people.
This stands in sharp contrast to the australopithecines and
perhaps Homo habilis, in which males tended to be much
larger than females. (McHenry 1996) In ape species that
exhibit a similar degree of sexual dimorphism, males
compete intensely for sexually receptive females, and
male-female relationships tend to be transitory and non-
cooperative. The reduced size difference in H[omo] ergaster
may signal the onset of a more typically human pattern, in
which male-male competition was more muted and male-
female relationships were more lasting and mutually
supportive. (89-92)

Klein concludes:

The emergence of Homo ergaster 1.8-1.7 million years ago
marked a watershed, for H. ergaster was the first hominin
species whose anatomy and behavior fully justify the label
human. … The evidence suggests that H. ergaster was the
first hominin species to resemble historic hunter-gatherers
not only in a fully terrestrial lifestyle, but also in a social
organization that featured economic cooperation between
males and females and perhaps between semipermanent
male-female units. (121)

Frans de Waal, perhaps surprisingly given his fascination
with ribald bonobos (see Chapter 5), is quite adamant on
the question of an original and uninterrupted human pattern of a male-dominated, "nuclear" family:

Human social organization is characterized by a unique
combination of (1) male bonding, (2) female bonding, and
(3) nuclear families. We share the first with chimpanzees,
the second with bonobos, and the third is ours alone. It's
no accident that people everywhere fall in love, are
sexually jealous, know shame, seek privacy, look for

father-figures in addition to mother-figures, and value
stable partnerships. The intimate male-female relationship
implied in all of this, which zoologists have dubbed a
"pair-bond," is bred into our bones. ...
   The size difference between the sexes, combined with
excellent cooperation among males makes it likely that
male dominance has always characterized our lineage,
and so inheritance likely followed paternal lines. (113-114)

Richard Leakey in *The Origin of Humankind*, while
not directly addressing the question of a male-dominated,
"nuclear" family, does endorse the idea of original patrilineal descent:

> Very probably, early Homo males remained in their natal
> groups with their brothers and half brothers, while the
> females transferred to other groups. (54)

These authors, and many other contemporary writers,
accept much of the tableau of interminable patriarchal "nuclear" families painted by the dominant, bourgeois school
of 20th-century anthropology that we discussed at the beginning of this work. In Chapter 8, we'll examine the anti-
communist basis for this entrenched defense of patriarchy,
but first we'll summarize the views of joint authors Christopher Ryan and Cacilda Jethá, who offer a book-length
analysis of human sexuality that concurs remarkably with
Johann Jakob Bachofen and Lewis Henry Morgan's notion
of primordial promiscuity.

CHAPTER 7

Challenging patriarchal puritanism

In Chapter 4, we quoted Engels' concise character-ization of social/sexual relations among our pre-class forebears as earlier theorized by Bachofen and Morgan. Let's review those words here:

> The study of primitive history … reveals conditions where the men live in polygamy [multiple wives] and their wives in polyandry [multiple husbands] at the same time, and their common children are therefore considered common to them all. (96)

So it would appear that there was evidence available, even in Engels' time, to support what must have been then and is even now, a most sexually provocative generalization about our ancestors.

Since the time when Engels penned that brief description, little attention has been paid to it from what this writer has been able to determine. Or perhaps, the words and their im-plications for contemporary society have simply been stu-diously avoided. Engels was not describing serial monoga-my, as some Marxist scholars have misconstrued. What his words imply for our species' sexuality is more fully elabo-rated in a recent, book length literary effort.

In the present writer's opinion, a debt of gratitude is owed to authors Christopher Ryan and Cacilda Jethá for their popularly written challenge to the global tyranny of what could be called patriarchal sex phobia. **Sex at Dawn**, their extensive overview of contemporary evidence for the promiscuous behavior of pre-agricultural humans, serves as a refreshing antidote to the all-too-common tendency of social science scholars to avoid detailed explorations of the sexual side of human behavior.

Their evidence includes material from the fields of zoology, anthropology, psychology, anatomy and physiology, as well as a critical analysis of contemporary social/sexual culture.

In lieu of a necessarily long summary of that evidence, the zoological portion of which parallels some of the material in this book's Chapter 5, we'll content ourselves with some of the generalizations they posit in the book's "Introduction":

> In the following pages, we reassess some of the most important science of our time. We question the deepest assumptions brought to contemporary views of marriage, family structure, and sexuality — issues affecting each of us every day and every night.
>
> We'll show that human beings evolved in intimate groups where almost everything was shared – food, shelter, protection, child care, even sexual pleasure. … we'll demonstrate that contemporary culture misrepresents the link between love and sex. With and without love, a casual sexuality was the norm for our prehistoric ancestors. (6)

Further along they write:

> As we'll explore in detail, before the advent of agriculture a hundred centuries ago, women typically had as much access to food, protection, and social support as did men. …
>
> Universal, culturally imposed sharing was simply the most effective way for our highly social species to minimize risk. …

Several types of evidence suggest our pre-agricultural (prehistoric) ancestors lived in groups where most mature individuals would have had several ongoing sexual relationships at any given time. Though often casual, these relationships were not random or meaningless. Quite the opposite: they reinforced crucial social ties holding these highly interdependent communities together.

We've found overwhelming evidence of a decidedly casual, friendly prehistory of human sexuality echoed in our own bodies, in the habits of remaining societies still lingering in relative isolation, and in some surprising corners of contemporary Western culture. (8-10)

'Who's Your Daddies?'

To give the reader at least a small sample of their insights in the field of psychology, here is their take in the chapter titled "Who's Your Daddies?" on the absence of sexual jealousy among hunter-gatherer men. Citing numerous anthropological sources, they write:

> Like mothers everywhere, a woman from these societies is eager to give her child every possible advantage in life. To this end, she'll typically seek out sex with an assortment of men. She'll solicit "contributions" from the best hunters, the best storytellers, the funniest, the kindest, the best-looking, the strongest, and so on — in the hopes her child will literally absorb the essence of each. ...
>
> Rather than being shunned ... children of multiple fathers benefit from having more than one man who takes a special interest in them. ...
>
> Far from being enraged at having his genetic heritage called into question, a man in these societies is likely to feel gratitude to other men for pitching in to help create and then care for a stronger baby. Far from being blinded by jealousy as the standard narrative predicts, men in these societies find themselves bound to one another by shared

paternity for the children they've fathered together. (91-92)

And further along:

> Paternity certainty, far from being the universal and over-riding obsession of all men everywhere and always, as the standard narrative insists, was likely a nonissue to men who lived before agriculture and resulting concerns with passing property through lines of paternal descent. (104)

These authors are, in no sense, Marxists. They have, however, a scientific, which is to say, a materialist, though not dialectical, approach to their subject. One cautionary for the reader intrigued enough to want to read their book: the writing is, in this writer's opinion, marred somewhat by a misplaced effort to flavor their text with witticisms.

More importantly, though, with a reformist rather than a revolutionary approach to social change through class struggle, what they offer in conclusion — a hopefully continued loosening of present-day social/sexual mores — ignores the crucial importance of the family under capitalism. The individual family, in all its present-day manifestations (two-parent, single-parent, homosexual parents, childless, common law) functions as the leaky lifeboat to which working-class and oppressed people must cling to save themselves from economic disaster. Lacking family support, many hundreds of thousands of homeless adults, elders and children languish and sometimes perish on the streets of U.S. cities at the present time.

Here's what Marx and Engels have to say about the patriarchal family in *The Communist Manifesto*:

> Abolition of the family! Even the most radical flair up at this infamous proposal of the Communists.

> On what foundation is the present family, the bourgeois family, based? On capital, on private gain. In its completely developed form this family exists only among the bourgeoisie. …
>
> The bourgeois family will vanish as a matter of course … with the vanishing of capital. (53)

Only with the establishment of worldwide communism will the solutions to the social/sexual discontents of class society be found. Only then will it be possible for the social/sexual freedom enjoyed by our hominin ancestors to be re-established. And to reach that end will involve mass struggle against the planet's present-day ruling classes, not the wishful thinking with which these authors conclude their otherwise noble effort.

Bronze sculpture of Karl Marx and Friedrich Engels at Alexanderplatz in the city of Berlin, Germany.

CHAPTER 8

The anti-communist basis of the anthropological counterrevolution

We've already made reference to the ideological counterrevolution of the early 20th century that sought to banish from bourgeois academia and popular capitalist culture the materialist and evolutionary perspective introduced by Lewis Henry Morgan and Frederick Engels in their anthropologically based writings.

This fierce attack on an important scientific discovery and, actually, on the science of anthropology itself, has a class basis in the historic struggle between the world's working class and the imperialist ruling class of the colonizing countries.

The essential nature of this struggle is capsulized in this often-quoted passage by Karl Marx and Frederick Engels in *The German Ideology*:

> The ideas of the ruling class are in every epoch the ruling ideas, i.e., the class which is the ruling material force of society, is at the same time its ruling intellectual force. (64)

In her groundbreaking 1971 booklet, Dorothy Ballan elaborated on this important point as it applies to the struggle over the direction that anthropology should take in the 20th century.

> More than anything else, the ruling class hates a consistent and irreconcilable view of social evolution. The reason

for this lies precisely in the fact that social evolution shows that capitalism, too, is merely a transitional stage of evolution of humanity from lower to higher stages — which incidentally includes the doom of their own dear free enterprise (capitalist) system. (40)

Marxist anthropologist Chris Knight has presented a carefully researched, comprehensive and provocative work on early human societies with his book **Blood Relations**. It includes a detailed description of the origins of the historical materialist school of anthropology and the subsequent wholesale assault on it by academic defenders of capitalist ruling-class interests.

Knight writes:

> The first anthropologists were social philosophers. Hobbes, Rousseau and Comte presented what would nowadays be called "anthropological" theories of human nature — as did [Karl] Marx, whose *Economic and Philosophic Manuscripts* … and *The German Ideology* … covered such topics as the nature of labor, the emergence of human language and the origins of the family.
>
> It was a range of interests shared by Lewis Henry Morgan, the American radical business lawyer who is often regarded as the principal founder of kinship studies and of anthropology in its modern sense. In the mid-nineteenth century, Morgan discovered the "classificatory" system of kinship terminology among the Iroquois Indians, and from this and much other evidence concluded that human society had everywhere evolved from communistic beginnings. (56)

The ruling class rallies academicians against social evolution

Knight characterized the attacks on the social evolutionist founders of anthropology as "the culturalist reaction":

The war years from 1914 to 1918 were the great intellectual buffers into which the idea of "progress" ran. … Almost simultaneously, in England, France, Germany and the United States, there arose schools of anthropology which … "in one way or another rejected the scientific mandate." It came to be widely believed that anthropology could never discover the origins of institutions or explain their causes. In Britain, "evolutionism" became not merely unfashionable but effectively outlawed. In the United States, the dominant school flatly asserted that there were no historical laws and that there could not be a science of history. (58)

Poster
USSR,
1920

Knight doesn't comment on the fact, but it is hardly a coincidence that this very period witnessed the appearance on the world stage of a fundamentally new social and political formation: the Soviet Union. The title of John Reed's magnificent account of the October 1917 Bolshevik Revolution in Russia, *Ten Days That Shook the World*, accurately characterized the impact of that profound event on the world, both on its workers and on its capitalist rulers.

Workers on every populated continent initiated plans to imitate the historic achievement of the Russian workers and peasants. The world's rich rulers, on the other hand, "shook," or perhaps more accurately, trembled! Their immediate response at the ideological level was to redouble their efforts to denigrate the great victory of the Russian workers and, more generally, to tighten their ideological control over the petty bourgeois intellectual leaders of the day, many of whom were initially taken with the power and moral authority of the growing worldwide communist movement that the Bolshevik victory inspired.

Academicians profess allegiance to imperialism

Lest anyone question whether the leading anthropologists of the great capitalist institutions of higher learning "got the message," Knight's exposition clearly reveals the openly reactionary political leanings expressed by some of the best-known of these very well remunerated academicians:

> When Franz Boas [German-American anthropologist (1858-1942), sometimes called "the father of American anthropology"] attacked the search for laws of history, he linked Social Darwinism in this respect with the view that "social structure is determined by economic forms" — an obvious reference to Marxism. (61)

Knight also quotes Robert Lowie, an Austrian-born U.S. anthropologist (1883-1957):

> Lowie … was politically aware enough to note how Morgan had become identified with Marxism in the eyes of anthropologists of his generation. "By a freak of fortune," Lowie observed, Morgan "has achieved the widest international celebrity of all anthropologists." This was "naturally" not due to Morgan's solid achievements "but to a historical accident": his *Ancient Society* (1877) attracted the notice of Marx and Engels, who accepted and popularized its evolutionary doctrines as being in harmony with their own philosophy. (61-62)

Knight reports how Lowie found it surprising that:

> "German workingmen would sometimes reveal an uncanny familiarity with the Hawaiian and Iroquois mode of designating kin [subjects about which Morgan had written], matters not obviously connected with a proletarian revolution."

Lowie went on to note that Morgan "has been officially canonized by the present Russian regime," whose spokesmen declare his work "of paramount importance for the materialistic analysis of primitive communism." (62)

The prolific French anthropologist and ethnologist, Claude Levi-Strauss (1908-2009), was not to be left out of this counterrevolutionary chorus:

> [He] earnestly assured his readers that … "we have been careful to eliminate all historical speculation, all research into origins, and all attempts to reconstruct a hypothetical order in which institutions succeeded one another … We do not know … and never shall know, anything about the first origins of beliefs and customs the roots of which plunge into a distant past." (68)

Knight summarizes:

The main and overriding aim was to root out Morgan's notion of "primitive communism" and to discredit Engels' *The Origin of the Family, Private Property and the State*. So much was this the priority, that on both sides of the Atlantic [anthropologists of the dominant schools] were quite capable of resorting to arguments about "origins" themselves — usually in throw-away remarks or casual asides — whenever it served their polemical purposes. It was as if they were warning their students and readers not to investigate such questions too closely, yet claiming to be unafraid of the consequences should such warnings be defied — after all, even if research into origins were to be carried out, Marx, Morgan and Engels would surely be found to be wrong! (69)

Anthropological accomplices to colonial enslavers

Of related interest are the revealing words of several British anthropologists with regard to their attempts to help their nation's imperialist leaders resist their declining colonial fortunes following World War I:

As [Alfred] Radcliffe-Brown [an English social anthropologist (1881-1955)] put it, anthropology "has an immediate practical value in connection with the administration and education of backward peoples [sic]." (64)

[Bronislaw] Malinowski frequently warned that educated African "agitators" and nationalists should be understood and if possible won over to European aims lest "by ignoring them and treating them with contempt we drive them into the open arms of world-wide Bolshevism." (67)

To complete this section on the nauseatingly class-collaborationist and racist subservience of some of the best-known anthropologists of the 20th century, let's return briefly to the 1931 debate between Malinowski and Briffault that was featured in Chapter 1.

In full hearing of a BBC radio audience, Malinowski was at least as anxious to exhibit his anti-communist credentials as he was to assert the eternal verity of patriarchal, one-man/one-woman marriage. Malinowski wasted no time setting the political tone of his presentation:

> Let us have a look at the facts all around us. Most startling of all, we have, in Soviet Russia, revolutionary experiments on a vast scale. Here a number of remarkable enactments have modified the juridical character of marriage almost out of recognition. Marriage, in the eyes of the law, has completely ceased to be a religious institution. It has almost ceased to be a legal contract. It is regarded as a sociological fact. Marriage comes into being when two people of opposite sex decide to live together, to share a household, to co-operate economically. …
>
> Communist marriage is thus, in the eyes of the law, a perfectly free and voluntary arrangement. Adultery is not a legal offence. Bigamy is not punishable by law. In juridical theory it is, therefore, possible in Soviet Russia to establish what the sociologist calls "group marriages" or communal unions. That is to say, several men and several women may run a communal household, and indiscriminately share as much of their lives as they like. …
>
> If I were to add that Soviet law fully allows, not to say encourages, all practices of family limitation, that is, has made abortion legal, that there are no punishments for incest, some of you might be disgusted and scandalized, others, perhaps very enthusiastic. (Briffault 1956: 21-23)

Malinowski here offers a rather unenlightened and un-objective characterization of what was then occurring in the Soviet Union with regard to women's rights, family life and marriage. Between the choices of "scandal" and "enthusiasm," Malinowski was clearly counting on the former response on the part of most of his listeners as he sought to undermine Briffault's defense of what was considered the Marxist view of marriage and the family.

He might have added, in a final flourish in his effort to besmirch Briffault — by association — as devoid of any "moral" convictions, that one of the first acts of the Bolshevik government was to decriminalize homosexual behavior. (For the background and details of this historic first, see Leslie Feinberg's *Lavender and Red series*, Parts 8-10, at workers.org.)

CHAPTER 9

The significance of 'classificatory kinship'

In this chapter, we deal with Lewis Henry Morgan's crucial "classificatory kinship" discovery. Classificatory kinship patterns, described below, present a seeming conundrum that has alternately been puzzled over, dismissed or, for many years now, largely ignored by anthropologists of the bourgeois schools. Morgan, however, faced their reality head on and drew from their pervasive existence among foraging and hunting groups a provocative conclusion regarding early human social/sexual relations.

Lewis Morgan's 590-page *Systems of Consanguinity and Affinity of the Human Family* contains an extensive survey of kinship terms used by various Indigenous peoples of the Western Hemisphere, Asia, Africa, Oceania, Europe and the Near East. From an analysis of the recurring patterns that he found, he drew a profound conclusion.

'Classificatory' vs. 'descriptive' kinship

On page 143, Morgan elaborates on the distinction between "classificatory" and "descriptive" kinship terms:

> [In the classificatory system] my father's brother's son is my "brother" ... and I apply to him the same term I use to designate [my] own brother: the son of this collateral brother and the son of my own brother are both my "sons." And I apply to them the same term I would use to desig-

nate my own son. In other words, the person first named is admitted into the same relationship as my own brothers, and these last named as my own sons. The principle of classification is carried to every person in the several collateral lines, near and remote, in such a manner as to include them all in the several great classes. Although apparently arbitrary and artificial, the results produced by the classification are coherent and systematic. ...

As now used and interpreted, with marriage between single pairs actually existing, it is an arbitrary and artificial system, because it is contrary to the nature of descents, confounding relationships which are distinct, separating those which are similar, and diverting the streams of the blood from the collateral channels into the lineal. Consequently, it is the reverse of the descriptive system. It is wholly impossible to explain its origin on the assumption of the existence of the family founded upon marriage between single pairs; but it may be explained with some degree of probability on the assumption of the antecedent existence of a series of customs and institutions, one reformatory of the other, commencing with promiscuous intercourse and ending with the establishment of the family, as now constituted, resting upon marriage between single pairs.

Morgan was, it now appears, overly cautious in drawing this conclusion, using the phrase "with some degree of probability." In the almost century and a half since the appearance of *Systems*, no one has advanced a clearer or more parsimonious explanation for the prevalence of classificatory kinship terms among Indigenous peoples.

Forms of address under the classificatory system

What might be termed "the collective mind-set" of the classificatory system users is also revealed in the forms of address they use and the reluctance they feel toward the use of personal names. Morgan writes in **Systems**:

> The American Indians always speak to each other, when related, by the term of relationship, and never by the personal name of the person addressed. In familiar intercourse, and in formal salutation, they invariably address each other by the exact relationship of consanguinity or affinity in which they stand related. I have put the question direct to native Indians of more than fifty different nations, in most cases at their villages or encampments, and the affirmance of this usage has been the same in every instance. Over and over again it has been confirmed by personal observation. When it is considered that the number of those who are bound together by the recognized family ties is several times greater than amongst ourselves, where remote collateral relatives are practically disowned, the necessity for each person to understand the system through all its extent to enable him to address his kinsmen by the conventional term of relationship becomes at once apparent. It is not only the custom to salute by kin, but an omission to recognize in this manner a relative, would, amongst most of these nations, be a discourtesy amounting to an affront. In Indian society the mode of address, when speaking to a relative, is the possessive form of the term of relationship; e.g., *my father, my elder brother, my grandson, my nephew, my niece, my uncle, my son-in-law, my brother-in-law,* and so on throughout the recognized relationships. If the parties are not related, then *my friend.* The effect of this custom in imparting as well as preserving a knowledge of the system through all of its ramifications is sufficiently obvious. There is another custom which renders this one a practical necessity. From some cause, of which it is not necessary here to seek an explanation, an American Indian is reluctant to mention his own personal name. It would be

a violation of good manners for an Indian to speak to another Indian by his name. If I ask one to tell me his name he will probably comply with my request after a moment's hesitation, because, as an American, the question is not singular from me; but, even then, if he has a companion with him, the latter will at once relieve him from embarrassment by answering in his place. In repeated instances I have verified this peculiarity in widely separated localities. This reserve in the use of personal names has tended to prevent the relaxation of the usage of addressing by kin, whilst, at the same time, it has contributed powerfully to the knowledge and maintenance of the system. (132-133)

'All things ... change'

Dorothy Ballan's insightful 1971 booklet, *Feminism and Marxism*, gave a succinct and accurate explanation of how and why Marxism is such a powerful tool in the investigation of human history and prehistory:

> Marxism teaches that all things in nature and society are in constant, uninterrupted and everlasting change. Nothing is eternal; everything has a beginning, goes through a period of development, growth and decadence, and ultimately a transformation into other forms. And that, of course, applies no less to the development of the family. (6)

And, we might add, to the institution of marriage.

Chris Knight, a contemporary Marxist anthropologist, revisits Morgan's discovery in a paper titled "Early Human Kinship Was Matrilineal." (In Allen, Callan, Dunbar and James 2008: 61-82)

Taking up Bronislaw Malinowski's criticism of Morgan's discovery, in which Malinowski claimed that "the facts of kinship would always turn out to be (a) biological and (b) individual," Knight counters:

> Classificatory kinship is anything but "individual." …
> It is the kind of kinship we would expect if bonds of
> siblinghood consistently prevailed over marital ties. Let
> me be more precise. It is the kind of kinship we would
> expect if groups of sisters drew on support from brothers
> in periodically standing up to husbands — a reproductive
> strategy aimed at enhancing female bargaining power and
> driving up male mating effort. … For obvious reasons,
> opposite-sex siblings cannot always "stand in" for one
> another in quite the same straightforward way as same-sex
> siblings. But where kinship is classificatory, sibling unity
> in general is accorded primacy over marital bonds. (62)

In this paper, Knight also explores some further ramifications that are suggested by classificatory kinship.

> Classificatory kinship doesn't operate on [a] myopic scale.
> Its premises are not those of Western competitive
> individualism. Although it doesn't eliminate intimacy or
> individuality, classificatory kinship operates on a grander
> level — on which bonds of sisterhood and brotherhood
> create networks of interdependence, decisively overriding
> parochial attachments and aims. Contrary to Western
> prejudices, for example, no Aboriginal Australian
> hunter-gatherer could be said to have inhabited a
> "small-scale community."

As a demonstrative example, he quotes an anthropological report that concludes:

> "[An Aboriginal] native could, at least theoretically,
> traverse the entire continent, stopping at each tribal
> boundary to compare notes on relatives, and at the end
> of his journey know precisely whom in the local group
> he should address as grandmother, father-in-law, sister,
> etc., whom he might associate freely with, whom he must
> avoid, whom he might or might not have sexual relations
> with, and so on."

Establishing chains of connection stretching across thousands of miles, these [Australian] Aborigines' mathematically elegant section and subsection systems — logical extensions of the simple principle of sibling equivalence — were built to a scale quite beyond the conception of scholars familiar only with kinship in its truncated Western forms. (64)

Levirate/sororate marriage

Knight continues:

A further expression of the equivalence of siblings is the levirate (or sororate) — inheritance by a person of his or her deceased sibling's spouse. … In the levirate/sororate, a person steps into the marital role of a deceased sibling with little or no ceremony and as a matter of course. In a sense, the living sibling was "married" to the deceased's spouse already, since siblings are kin equivalents and marital contracts are arrangements not between private individuals but kin groups on either side. … To the extent that "classificatory" principles prevail — the logic implies that in each generation, those entering into relationships are neither individuals nor marital couples. They are self-organized coalitions of sisters/brothers. (64-65)

With regard to the prevalence of levirate/sororate marriage among foraging and hunting peoples, anthropologist Robert Lowie writes in *Primitive Society* that:

It is easier to count cases where the custom is positively known to be lacking than to enumerate instances of its occurrence. (32)

Knight touches on several other issues in his paper, concluding with his take on the material basis for matrilocality among forager/hunter groups.

Whether in Australia, Africa or the Americas, a young bridegroom must not only visit his bride in her camp but also work strenuously for her, surrendering to his in-laws whatever game he catches. This, after all, is the essence of "bride-service" — the fundamental economic institution in any hunter-gatherer society. ... Females, then, obtain the best deal when they remain following marriage with close kin. (80)

Knight has much more to say about what he terms the "conflicting demands" of the male and female members of the primordial hominin bands and clans. In the next few chapters, after an introduction to the important role of women in early human society and some background information on Chris Knight and Evelyn Reed, another Marxist scholar, we'll summarize their efforts to make sense of the many practices and beliefs of foraging and hunting groups, specifically involving relations between the sexes, to which most anthropologists have reacted with incomprehension and, often, disparagement. Both of these authors address the processes that are likely to have resulted in "modern" human culture, but with somewhat different hypotheses.

CHAPTER 10

More contemporary findings that support Engels' view

Our inclusion in this work of so much material that supports and enriches Engels' theory might, perhaps, be questioned either as unnecessary overkill or, alternatively, as an ill-advised effort to defend ideas that have usually been treated in bourgeois academic circles as pseudo-scientific Marxist dogma.

To the charge of overkill, we may be guilty. But our years of paging through the material we attempt to summarize in this work have constituted an exciting intellectual adventure, almost as exciting as our first reading of Engels' **Origin** way back when. We can only hope the reader will have a similarly stimulating experience.

As for this book constituting a defense of an important part of Marxist scientific theory, and a contribution toward the liberation of women, as well as men and LGBTQ2S people, we offer no apology. Patriarchal capitalism must go!

In this chapter, we present thumbnail reviews of a number of book length anthropological publications that have appeared in the last half century. While it will be impossible to offer more than a cursory look at some of the content of these works in the limited space of this chapter, a few brief notes on each might prove useful to the activist scholar seeking further printed material on this important topic.

62

Rayna Reiter's *Toward an Anthropology of Women*

Toward an Anthropology of Women is a collection of 17 essays, all authored by women and most by practicing anthropologists. In her "Introduction," editor Rayna Reiter argues:

> We need new studies that will focus on women; it cannot be otherwise because of the double bias which has trivialized and misinterpreted female roles for so long. (16)

Sampling just three of the essays in this collection, we start with "Woman the Gatherer: Male Bias in Anthropology." In this essay, Sally Slocum writes that:

> Too much attention has been given to the skills required by hunting, and too little to the skills required for gathering and the raising of dependent young. (46-47)

Hundreds of archaeologists have spent their professional lives studying bones, teeth and worked stones, the only remaining evidence of our hominin ancestors.

> If, however, instead of thinking in terms of tools and weapons, we think in terms of *cultural inventions*, a new aspect is presented. I suggest that two of the *earliest and most important* cultural inventions were containers to hold the products of gathering, and some sort of sling or net to carry babies. (Slocum's Italics; 46)

Patricia Draper begins her essay on "!Kung Women: Contrasts in Sexual Egalitarianism in and Sedentary Contexts" with the observation:

> Most members of the Harvard !Kung Bushman Study Project who have thought about the subject of !Kung women's status agree that !Kung society may be the least sexist of any we have experienced. (77)

Draper is referring to the !Kung or San people of the Kalahari Desert of southwestern Africa, a minority of whom still live by traditional methods of hunting and gathering.

These people "subsist primarily on wild vegetable foods and game meat. They are semi-nomadic." (79) In contrast:

> The great majority … have abandoned their traditional …
> way of life and are now living in sedentary and semi-
> squatter status in or near the villages of Bantu pastoralists
> and European ranchers. (79)

Draper provides much descriptive content to demonstrate the conditions of sexual equality that still exist among the !Kung who have remained foragers and hunters and how those conditions of equality have eroded with the adoption by other !Kung of sedentary living.

Gayle Rubin's "The Traffic in Women: Notes on the 'Political Economy' of Sex" operates at a more theoretical level. She takes on both Sigmund Freud, for his "Oedipus complex" construct, and Claude Levi-Strauss, for his "exchange of women" theory. Rubin's position is that:

> Gender is a socially imposed division of the sexes. It is
> a product of the social relations of sexuality. Kinship
> systems rest upon marriage. They therefore transform
> males and females into "men" and "women," each an
> incomplete half which can only find wholeness when
> united with the other. … The idea that men and women
> are more different from one another than either is from
> anything else must come from somewhere other than
> nature. … Far from being an expression of natural
> differences, exclusive gender identity is the suppression
> of natural similarities. It requires repression: in men,
> of whatever is the local version of "feminine" traits; in
> women, of the local definition of "masculine" traits.
> (179-180)

So we see, to Rubin's credit, that she touches on a subject rarely dealt with in anthropological texts:

Gender is not only an identification with one sex; it also entails that sexual desire be directed toward the other sex. The sexual division of labor is implicated in both aspects of gender — male and female it creates them, and it creates them heterosexual. The suppression of the homosexual component of human sexuality, and by corollary, the oppression of homosexuals, is therefore a product of the same system whose rules and relations oppress women. (180)

Martin and Voorhies' *Female of the Species*

Written in a very readable style, *Female of the Species*, by professors M. Kay Martin and Barbara Voorhies, spans the same lengthy time frame of primate and hominin existence as does the present effort and offers well thought out discussions of the changing roles of women through prehistory and history. What we found of special interest for our purposes is their statistical analysis of the importance of gathering in 90 contemporary societies.

They are careful to underscore the limitations of their findings based on the character of the societies studied:

It is important to remember … that all modern foragers are acculturated to a greater or lesser degree. In addition, all have experienced an enforced alteration of their natural and social environments. … These modern representatives occupy generally undesirable and non-productive habitats, and are subsequently less populous and less complex than even their most immediate ancestors. Our interest in contemporary foragers remains, however, because they have been so systematically utilized in evolutionist and androcentric theory, and more simply because they provide the only examples of preagricultural adaptations available for direct observation. (180-181)

Their findings include the fact that, among their 90 sample societies, the great majority depend on hunting for only 30 to 40 percent of their diet. They conclude:

> The hunt is a much more precarious endeavor … than is the collection of nutritious stationary resources. It is because of this reason that the products of gathering traditionally compose the dietary staples. Since women are almost wholly responsible for the provision of these foodstuffs, their productive contribution in foraging societies is substantial indeed. (183)

Investigating the kinship/social structure of these 90 societies, the authors report that they are "overwhelmingly bilateral in descent." (184-185) This means that, as in contemporary capitalist societies, "descent is reckoned through both parents equally." (184) And, "the type of foraging society most strongly represented in the present sample is patrilocal in residence." (185) However:

> While these figures are instructive, caution must be exercised in their interpretation. The great majority of these data were compiled from ethnographic accounts written well after the conquest and subjugation of indigenous peoples. (185)

And further along they write:

> In nearly every documented case of alterations in the reckoning of unilineal descent during the postcontact period, the direction of this change has been from matrilineal to patrilineal. Missionaries and early statesmen sometimes abhorred the matrilineal custom whereby a man devoted his primary responsibility to his *sister's* rather than his own children, and in many instances literally imposed upon males a role more in keeping with Western European values. (Martin and Voorhies' italics; 186)

Frances Dahlberg's *Woman the Gatherer*

The scientific papers brought together by anthropologist Frances Dahlberg under the title *Woman the Gatherer* were, at least in part, in response to a 1966 conference and subsequent 1968 publication, both carrying the title *Man the Hunter.* (Lee and Devore 1968)

In her Preface to the studies, editor Dahlberg comments:

> Although [the Man the Hunter conference] did not omit women, it occurred before the women's movement had revitalized the study of women in anthropology. (ix)

Summarizing the content of *Woman the Gatherer*, she writes:

> Taken together, the six contributions add woman the mate chooser, woman the mother, woman the aunt, woman the communicator, woman the power, woman the ritual actor, and woman the hunter to woman the gatherer. (x-xi)

Among the offerings in *Woman the Gatherer*, we were particularly impressed by Adrienne Zihlman's contribution, directly challenging, as it does, the idea that male hominin hunting was the key factor in hominin evolutionary success. In the collection's Chapter 2, "Women as Shapers of Human Adaptation," Zihlman draws on comparative information of great ape behavior and the existing hominin fossil record.

Following an extended discussion of body size dimorphism and canine tooth size among common and pygmy chimpanzees (bonobos) and early hominins, Zihlman concludes:

> Canine tooth size may be more helpful in inferring social behavior. The fact that they are small and nondimorphic [no size difference between males and females] among early hominids could reflect sociability among individuals, between males and females, females and females, and a

reduction of male-male competition and aggression, similar to, and even an extension of, that found among pygmy chimpanzees [bonobos]. This behavioral interpretation of an anatomical character fits with two hypotheses presented in this chapter and discussed by others regarding early human social life: 1) Food sharing has long been considered a new and integral part of economic and social life of the human species. ... [and] 2) With regard to kin investment by males, females preferred as sexual partners those males who were more social and less aggressive toward them and who contributed to the welfare of their own kin group. (102)

Regarding the significance of hunting for early humans, Zihlman begins by noting the need for a clear definition:

Human hunting, as we know it, is a composite of behaviors: stalking, pursuing, bringing down, killing, and butchering, and various tools are tied in with some parts. (105)

Following a discussion of these various components, she writes:

Questions remain regarding the emergence of hunting but the gap narrows when we recognize the continuity and similarities between gathering and hunting. Gathering may have laid the social and technological foundations for the emergence of hunting. (108)

As pre-existing bases for the introduction of hunting, she suggests the existence of sharing patterns already established between mothers and offspring, the employment of tools initially invented for gathering activities, the adaptation of social features of small animal gathering activities, and the techniques developed for and the knowledge gained from the butchering of the scavenged carcasses of larger animals.

Capsulizing the conclusions that can be drawn from the other reports in this collection, ethnographic material on the Agta people of eastern Luzon, the Australian Aborigines, the central African Mbutis and the Chipewyan people of Canada, Dahlberg writes:

> The chapters of this book do not support the idea that women are valued less than men because of the restrictions of maternity or because of differential economic contributions. … Research that starts with the majority — women and children — does not support a legend of man the hunter or woman the gatherer but leads to a more complicated story. An accurate reconstruction of early hominid life is still being fashioned, minus the high drama of man the hunter. (27)

Lori Hager's *Women in Human Evolution*

In "Sex and Gender in Paleoanthropology," Lori D. Hager's contribution to **Women in Human Evolution**, a collection of essays penned by female scientists which she edited, Hager describes a public exhibit on human biology and evolution at New York City's American Museum of Natural History.

> We see "Lucy" and her "mate" walking across the plains of Tanzania, implying that these hominids are responsible for the footprints at Laetoli (even though "Lucy" was found thousands of miles away in Ethiopia!). We see "Lucy" with a larger male walking beside her, his arm around her shoulders, protecting and comforting her. (15)

Reviewing a large amount of scientific data relating to methods of determination of sex among fossil specimens, Hager shows that whether "Lucy" was male or female remains in question. However, the sexist subtext of the Natural History Museum exhibit, which she doesn't address, is that females, even going back to 3.2 million years ago, have always been the "weaker sex."

Alison Wylie's essay, "Good Science, Bad Science, or Science as Usual," includes a choice example of "scientific" sexism by none other than famed anthropologist Claude Lévi-Strauss from his field journal in the 1930s:

> The entire village left the next day in about thirty canoes, leaving us alone in the abandoned houses with the women and children. (45)

The essays by Dean Falk ("Brain Evolution in Females"), Susan Sperling and Yewoubdar Beyene ("A Pound of Biology and a Pinch of Culture or a Pinch of Biology and a Pound of Culture?"), and Camilla Power and Leslie Aiello ("Female Proto-Symbolic Strategies") are equally fascinating but highly technical and thus too much of a challenge for this writer to attempt to summarize, but well worth a careful read.

Cueva de las Manos (Spanish for Cave of Hands) is a cave or a series of caves located in the province of Santa Cruz, Argentina. The art in the cave dates from 13,000 to 9,000 years ago.

Lascaux, France, cave painting c. 15,000 B.C.E. A forensic expert determined that people of all ages and both sexes were making the early art found in caves, not just senior male shamans.

CHAPTER II

Eleanor Leacock's
Myths of Male Dominance

Eleanor Burke Leacock is perhaps best known for her superbly thoughtful and clarifying "Introduction" to the 1972, International Publishers edition of *Origin of the Family, Private Property and the State*. Her unstinting, well-reasoned support for Engels' discoveries took real courage in the climate of anti-communism that still prevailed at that time in academia and elsewhere in the heartland of world imperialism.

But if a single volume were to be recognized as providing the most valuable contemporary support for Engels' profound theses in *Origin*, we would nominate Leacock's *Myths of Male Dominance* for consideration.

Leacock, who died at the age of 64 in 1987, suffered professionally both as a woman in an academic field (anthropology) dominated by men and as a Marxist in the profoundly anti-communist climate that then and now dominates the U.S. educational system as well as imperialist culture in general. In the "Preface" to *Myths,* she credits the women's movement of the late 1960s and early 1970s for her appointment as chair of the anthropology department at the City College of New York after many years of poorly paid, often part-time teaching positions.

Myths is a collection of her essays that fall neatly into four groupings plus an introduction. In the "Introduction," she makes explicit her historical perspective and political orientation:

> As Marx pointed out, it was the expansion of the European market into the world market that transformed mercantile Europe into capitalist Europe. Historically, then, capitalism has been inseparable from racist brutality and national oppression throughout its history. … [Marx] revealed the process whereby direct relations among people, as they labored to produce and to exchange the goods they then consumed, were transformed by the emergence of commodity production for profit, so that people's very labor became an alien force against them. (13-14)

The centrality of racism
in the development of capitalism

In outlining the historical context of capitalist development, Leacock seeks to expose the serious distortion of Marxism that separates racial, national, sexual and gender oppression from the class struggle and, in doing so, minimizes their significance:

> It is as if the victory of bourgeois market relations over feudalism, and the "freeing" of workers to sell their labor, were largely internal European developments that involved only white men. In fact, it was the uniting of class, race, and national exploitation and oppression on a world scale that made the triumph of the European bourgeoisie possible. The reality was all too painfully evident to Toussaint L'Ouverture when he unsuccessfully tried to win support for a free Haiti from the revolutionary French bourgeoisie, as C.L.R. James so masterfully relates [in his book *The Black Jacobins*]. (16)

She continues:

> Racism did, and still does, serve powerfully to divide the world's workers. … The point I want to make here is that the same is true when it comes to the oppression of women. And sex oppression goes further back, not just to the rise of capitalist class relations, but to the origins of class itself. (16)

The Montagnais-Naskapi people of Labrador

The essays in Part I deal with the Montagnais-Naskapi people of Labrador. Part II, titled "Social Evolution: From Egalitarianism to Oppression," includes a very detailed review and evaluation of Lewis Morgan's *Ancient Society*. Part III is an analysis and refutation of the prevailing view of timeless male pre-eminence. In the scant 12 pages of Part IV, she makes her anti-patriarchal, anti-capitalist political position crystal clear.

What makes Leacock's defense of Engels so powerful is her own highly perceptive, scientific observations among the Montagnais-Naskapi in her role as an anthropological field worker, and her scholarly digging into the extensive and largely disapproving observations of these natives of the Labrador Peninsula made by French Catholic missionaries more than three centuries earlier and recorded in the seventy-one volumes of *The Jesuit Relations and Allied Documents* (Thwaites 1899).

> [The good Jesuit priest, Père Le Jeune] lived with a Montagnais band in the winter of 1633-1634, and his accounts give a picture of their life in the days when they depended on hunting, not only for food, but for everything from clothes to snowshoe-webbing. Three or four families, usually related, lived together in a single large tent; men, women, and children travelled together, each working and contributing to the group to the extent he or she was able. …

Within the group, the social ethic called for generosity, cooperation, and patience, and Le Jeune commented on the good humor, the lack of jealousy, and the willingness to help that characterized daily life. Those who did not contribute their share were not respected, and it was a real insult to call a person stingy. (34)

Le Jeune found certain aspects of Montagnais social relations very troubling. Leacock cites a passage from *The Jesuit Relations:*

"The inconstancy of marriages and the facility with which they divorce each other, are a great obstacle to the Faith of Jesus Christ. We do not dare baptize the young people because experience teaches us that the custom of abandoning a disagreeable wife or husband has a strong hold on them." (50)

Leacock documents in detail the struggles of the Christian missionaries, playing out over several centuries, to impose their contrary values on the Montagnais and the effects that fur trading with the European invaders had on the formerly communal economy of the Indigenous peoples, and particularly, on the formerly egalitarian relations between men and women.

In a summary statement, she reports:

At the same time that the fur trade [with Europeans] was undercutting the foundation for Montagnais-Naskapi values and interpersonal ethics, the terrible scourge of epidemic disease, the escalation (or introduction) of warfare, and the delusion of relief from anxiety offered by alcohol were also undermining Montagnais-Naskapi self-assurance. (58-59)

Nevertheless, she concludes:

When I was there, conditions in the north woods were still such that the traditional Montagnais-Naskapi ethic of cooperativeness, tolerance, and non-punitiveness remained strong. (60)

Communal matrilocality

Leacock's take on the issue of communal matrilocality, the idea that husbands moved in with the wife's family, and women's power in general, is of interest. She suggests that:

> Probably the Jesuit recorders exaggerated this Montagnais-Naskapi pattern so different from their own. Reading backwards from the tenor of Montagnais life today, family decisions were probably a joint affair. … We should perhaps assume a similar exaggeration with respect to postmarital residence, for it is most unlikely that matrilocality was formerly universal among the Montagnais any more than patrilocality is today. (66)

Further along she writes:

> Constant movement was so characteristic of these Indians that the terms "patrilocality" or "matrilocality" are somewhat of a misnomer. Ties to territories were of minimal importance; the emphasis was on maintaining loving and compatible working groups. These were built both through conjugal and affinal relations, and, apparently, through pure friendships as well. (71)

She elaborates on the last point in Part II:

> My own view is that patrilocality is a post-contact phenomenon and that, before the era of trade, hunting bands were flexible in this regard, but tended toward *matrilocality*.

And on the matter of lineage:

> *Matrilineality* and *patrilineality* [tracing descent through the mother or the father, respectively] are often misnomers for band society, since their formal kinship organization is commonly minimal. (Leacock's italics; 112)

In the section of the book dealing with Lewis Henry Morgan's contributions, Leacock adds some further insightful thoughts on the issue of "lineality." (See below)

In a most revealing comment on pre-class politics, Leacock writes:

> As far as I could see, decision-making on ... important issues was a most subtle process — indeed an enigma to the [anthropological] fieldworker schooled in competitive hierarchies — whereby one found out how everybody concerned felt without committing oneself until one was fairly sure in advance that there would be common agreement. I was constantly struck by the elusive nature of the continual effort on the part of the Indians to operate together unanimously, but informally, in the direction of the greatest individual satisfaction without direct conflict of interest. The frustration this occasioned me as a field-worker will, I am sure, be familiar to those who have studied similar peoples. (71-72)

Louis Morgan's discovery

In Part II of *Myths*, Leacock contrasts anthropology's "endless isolated studies of limited phenomena" with Lewis Henry Morgan's discovery:

> As his material piled up, it yielded the profound and exciting discovery that kinship systems existed throughout the world which were similar to each other, but at marked variance with those known to Indo-European- and Semitic-speaking peoples. (87)

This discovery, as has previously been noted, was the material basis for a systematic theory of human social evolution.

She expresses disagreement with Morgan on several points, however:

> Unfortunately, many of the reasons for clan organization and matrilineality given by Morgan and other nineteenth century writers were erroneous, and this has clouded the issues. Certainty of biological parentage, one reason given for counting descent through women, is important to Western society, but of little importance in more egali-

tarian cultures. Morgan mentioned a greater natural desire on the part of women for sexual exclusiveness as instrumental in limiting the marriage group and laying the basis for clan organization, but there is no good cross-cultural evidence for this. He also believed the clan produced healthier people by limiting inbreeding. However, clan exogamy does not prohibit marriage of actual relatives. Cross-cousin marriage (marrying one's mother's brother's or father's sister's son or daughter, who are not members of one's own clan) is often a preferential match, since it has the unique advantage of strengthening already close ties … while at the same time building alliances across different clan groups. (113)

Leacock also reviews the stages posited by Morgan in the evolution of the human family and finds them, in fact, not supported by his own evidence. Her overriding concern is that:

To propose loose monogamy (with occasional polygamy) as having always been found among gathering-hunting peoples could mean to accept a commonly held view that the monogamous family is universal as the basic unit of society, that variations from culture to culture are relatively superficial, that, in short, there have not been qualitatively different forms of the family in human history. This view is, however, erroneous. … Among gathering-hunting peoples, the married pair and their children are in no sense the basic unit of society as they are in contemporary class-structured society. The band, not the family, is the collective, whether several families share a tipi or other dwelling, or whether the camp is a series of small lean-tos, wickiups, or other such casual shelters. Care and responsibility for the young, the old, and the infirm is not an individual matter, but social, the concern of the entire group, in a direct and unquestioned fashion. (125)

It is crucial to the organizations of women for their liberation to understand that it is the monogamous family as an economic unit, at the heart of class society, that is basic to their subjugation. Such understanding makes clear that childbearing itself is not responsible for the low status of women. … And more important, it indicates the way in which working-class women, not only in their obviously basic fight on the job but also in their seemingly more conservative battles for their families around schools, housing, and welfare, are actually posing a more basic challenge than that of the radicals. By demanding that society assume responsibility for their children, they are attacking the nature of the family as an economic unit, the basis of their own oppression and a central buttress of class exploitation. (307)

Personal autonomy

The Jesuit documents made clear to Leacock that among these hunting and foraging people at the very beginning of the European invasion:

Individuals within Naskapi society were autonomous; people made decisions about activities for which they were responsible. Group decisions were arrived at through feeling for consensus. The essential and direct interdependence of the group as a whole both necessitated this autonomy and made it possible as a viable system — *total interdependence was inseparable from real autonomy.* … The emphasis was on generosity, on cooperation, on patience and good humor, but also on never forcing one's will on others. This ethic was enforced through ridicule and teasing, often bawdy, behind which lay the threat of great anger at injustice, and the deep fear of starvation, that might ultimately force individual hunters to abandon the group in order that someone might survive. (Leacock's italics; 21-22)

In a later section of the book, she elaborates on some of the social implications arising from personal autonomy among the Naskapi and other egalitarian band societies:

> Consensus, freely arrived at, within and among multifamily units was both essential to everyday living and possibly has implications that we do not usually confront. Individual autonomy was a necessity, and autonomy as a valued principle persists to a striking degree among the descendants of hunter-gatherers. It was linked with a way of life that called for great individual initiative and decisiveness along with the ability to be extremely sensitive to the feelings of lodge-mates. ... Decision-making in this context calls for concepts other than ours of leader and led, dominant and deferent. (138)

On the social status of women:

> Nothing in the structure of egalitarian band societies necessitated special deference to men. There were no economic and social liabilities that bound women to be more sensitive to men's needs and feelings than vice versa. This is even true in hunting societies, where women did not furnish a major share of the food. (140-141)

Referencing the letters of Father Le Jeune in *Jesuit Relations*, she adds:

> Disputes and quarrels among spouses were virtually nonexistent ... since each sex carried out its own activities without "meddling" in those of the other. ... Noting that women had "great power," [Le Jeune] expressed his disapproval of the fact that men had no apparent inclination to make their wives "obey" them or enjoin sexual fidelity upon them. ... [Le Jeune] was also distressed by the sharp and ribald joking and teasing into which women entered along with the men. "Their language has the foul odor of the sewers," he wrote. (141)

Leacock offers an anecdote from *Jesuit Relations* that reveals a striking disparity in the views of Montagnais-Naskapi men and French men on the issue of paternity:

> When the missionary, Le Jeune, upbraided an Indian for "allowing" his wife such sexual freedom that he could not be sure his son was his own, the Montagnais retorted, "Thou hast no sense. You French people love only your own children, but we love all the children of our tribe." (228)

Leacock's own observations of Montagnais men several centuries later led her to report:

> Fathers participated in the care and socialization of children with an ease and spontaneity deemed "feminine" in our culture. (227)

When contemporary students of anthropology come across the observation that migrating and hunting groups sometimes left old people behind to die alone when the band moved on, or when these students encounter the assertion that many of these societies practiced infanticide, the predictable reaction is horrified condemnation. Yet both practices, understood from the point of view of the hunter-gatherers themselves, were eminently reasonable if the well-being of the collective was to be maintained. Leacock asserts that it was the infirm themselves who altruistically insisted on being abandoned on the basis that their special needs represented an intolerable burden that threatened the existence of the collective. Similarly:

> [C]hildren had to be spaced for their own well-being as well as that of their mothers and the group as a whole, and infanticide has to be understood as a last resort when various methods of birth control or abortion have failed. (227)

Leacock's *Myths* is rich in facts, persuasive argument and the application of Marxist theory. This brief delving into its richness is no substitute for a careful reading of the original work.

CHAPTER 12

Women and the struggle for human solidarity

For anthropologists who subscribe to an evolutionary materialist approach to human origins, the central role of the female of the species in the process of creating a distinctly human culture is beyond question. As the producers of new life, the mothers were crucial to the continuance of the collective. As the nurturers of the totally helpless human infants and as the caregivers, protectors and teachers of the young children, the women played the primary role in the enculturation of each new generation.

But there is much more to say about their importance in producing what Frederick Engels termed "the transition from ape to man." In his never-completed essay entitled *The Part Played by Labor in the Transition from Ape to Man*, Engels writes:

> First labor, after it and then with it, speech — these were
> the two most essential stimuli under the influence of
> which the brain of the ape gradually changed into that
> of man. (11)

Dependence on language as uniquely important to Homo sapiens and essential to our species' cultural transformation is indisputable. Clearly, as an extremely efficient and productive form of communication, its development involved the interaction of individuals of both sexes, but its introduction and its transmission to each new generation was certainly primarily the work of women.

The total helplessness of hominin babies and the extended nutritional dependence of hominin children would have necessitated the provisioning and sharing of food between the mother and her offspring on a broader scale than that witnessed among the other primates. Equally important, the collectivity of women and children would have constituted the social center of the primordial band. Women would have been keepers of the fire, producers of tools, builders of shelter and processors of food.

Our confidence in these assertions concerning the crucial role of hominin women rests, in part, on the patterns of life among forager and hunter groups as described in innumerable anthropological and related reports, especially those written by witnesses untainted by the anthropological counterrevolution discussed earlier.

Two outstanding Marxist scholars

In the views of two Marxist-oriented theoreticians of human origins, it was the collective intervention of women that introduced patterns of sociality, cooperation and sharing to the primordial hominin bands. Both Evelyn Reed and Chris Knight exhibit a breathtakingly comprehensive familiarity with existing ethnographic, anthropological and archeological findings. Their hypotheses regarding "the transition from ape to man" rest on the extensive use and interpretation of this knowledge.

Reed, a Marxist and a feminist activist who died in 1979, devoted 20 years to her study of the existing literature in the areas of ethnology, social anthropology, archeology, zoology and related fields. These two decades spent mulling over hundreds of field reports, theoretical compilations and other materials resulted in a remarkable document, the 491-page book titled *Woman's Evolution*.

Interestingly, and perhaps not surprisingly, we found only a single reference to Reed's book among the many, post *Woman's Evolution*, printed and online materials consulted in preparation for this book. We suspect that the culprit here is the anti-communist, good-old-boys network, more commonly referred to as the bourgeois academic establishment.

Reed was an anti-capitalist activist and women's liberation leader, not a bourgeois academician. Thus, she lacked the qualifications necessary to be taken seriously by the academic establishment. As a revolutionary socialist, she would have had difficulty earning the necessary credentials, had she even wanted to. Nevertheless, as we hope to demonstrate, at least in brief, her hypothesis is based on a solid foundation of scientific reports, objective evaluations and logical reasoning.

Knight, also a Marxist activist, is an anthropologist by profession. His theoretical contribution, *Blood Relations*, was referenced earlier in this work. It contains, in addition to Knight's take on the revolutionary intervention of prehistoric women, a comprehensive history of how the new science of anthropology was effectively de-evolutionized in the early 20th century.

Knight has admirable credentials as an activist. To the discredit of his superiors, he was first suspended and then fired from his academic position at the University of East London for his words and actions as a leader of an April 2009 protest in London against a G20 Summit of imperialist political leaders and bankers. Then, in 2011, he was arrested with 21 other "Occupy London" activists for targeting a mining company's criminal activities.

Deciphering past practices and beliefs

In the vast body of data addressing various aspects of the lives of foraging and hunting peoples, there are many seeming puzzles, oddities and sometimes utterly baffling practices and beliefs, at least as seen through the eyes of observers from the capitalist world. The assessments that explorers, slavers, missionaries, traders, entrepreneurs and other agents of the global imperialist system have made of these practices and beliefs have often smacked of blatant, colonialist-style racism. Anthropologists and ethnologists have not always been immune from similar disparagements.

A more neutral or disinterested response has been to write these practices and beliefs off as simply inexplicable, given the huge cultural gap between the peoples of the imperialist centers and those of the less-developed parts of the world. What both Reed and Knight have accomplished is to draw together some of the most poorly understood of these practices and beliefs, together with other factual information, to produce unifying concepts and parsimonious hypotheses that make sense of the data.

Of course, what we're most interested in is what their hypotheses have to say about prehistoric social/sexual relations and any clues concerning the origins of "marriage." But a short summary of each author's conceptual framework, although failing to provide a complete picture of its full power and scope, will at least delineate a context for the author's view of primordial social/sexual relations. We will tackle these challenges in the next two chapters.

CHAPTER 13

Domesticating the hunters — Reed's hypothesis

In Evelyn Reed's book, *Woman's Evolution*, she argues that the practice of cannibalism among male hominins during the millennia after they began hunting was a pervasive, destructive and potentially species-annihilating behavior. The survival of our hominin ancestors as a species was then secured by the intervention of the female members of the hominin bands, who set up cultural obstacles to inhibit this practice.

Cannibalism is, of course, an unsavory subject. Most people would opine that it is a rare phenomenon, a desperate response to the threat of starvation or a horror indulged in by unhinged sociopaths. It is, however, a behavior that has been observed among many contemporary primate species. It has also been documented among foraging and hunting groups. See, for example, the section on cannibalism in Lawrence Keeley's *War Before Civilization.* (103-106)

Reed's narrative is that the hominin meat-eating hunters didn't always distinguish between animals and the contending hominins from other bands whom they encountered. Fresh blood, whether the result of an animal kill or a struggle between two hominin bands, would have signaled an opportunity for a meal. Reed assumes that the foraging female hominins were completely or largely vegetarians, continuing the herbivore tradition of their tree-dwelling ancestors. This gustatory dichotomy may strike the reader as doubtful. However, Reed is able to cite both archeological and anthropological evidence for this proposition.

Archaeological findings that postdate Reed's book bolster her view. Summarizing the analysis of hominin bones found in Spain and Europe's Caucasus Mountains as well as in South Africa, Carole Travis-Henikoff writes in *Dinner with a Cannibal*:

> Stone-tool cut marks that correlate with de-fleshing and disarticulation, breakage of long bones for extraction of marrow, method of deposition of remains, along with other recognizable evidence, demonstrate the practice of cannibalism within the ranks of some of our oldest kin. ... Fossil and archaeological evidence from many caves on many continents imply that a great many of our forebears saw nothing wrong or shameful in the act of ingesting others of their own kind. (89-90)

The datings on the evidence she is referring to range between 1 million and 2 million years ago.

A reasonable assumption would be that the objects of early hominin cannibalism would be the casualties of fighting between hominin bands. But Reed argues that no distinction was originally made between animal and hominin prey, but that the great contribution of hominin women was the creation of cultural taboos that prevented the male hunters from occasionally eating their own kind or even their own kin.

Unraveling the 'totem and taboo' phenomenon

Reed has a refreshingly clear explanation of the purpose of the "totem and taboo" phenomenon, an aspect of the culture of forager/hunter societies whose significance has baffled many an anthropologist.

> The primitive institution of totemism and taboo … represents the earliest form of social control over food and sex hungers, classifying that which is forbidden in both realms. The sex clause is well known; under totemic law a man could not mate with any woman belonging to his totem-kin group. Under the food clause, a man was prohibited from killing or eating totem-kin animals. (23)

Elaborating on this idea, she writes:

> Unable to draw the dividing line between humans and animals through biological criteria, our earliest ancestors were obliged to invent other means for making the distinction. They did this through their social kinship system. This began as totem kinship before it evolved into the higher form, the classificatory system of kinship. Those who were of the same kin were the same kind, human beings. Outsiders, non-kin, were members of a different kind, i.e., animals. This kinship criterion established the boundaries of cannibalism. (30)
>
> The essence of the totemic taboo was that it eradicated any possibility that a kinsman would hunt, kill, or eat another kinsman. …
>
> Once instituted, totemism not only checked cannibalism but produced a broader beneficial effect. It tended to protect animal and plant life in general in a period when unregulated plunder of food supplies could have produced results almost as anti-social as cannibalism. (38)
>
> Those proto-human groups in which these controls were most effective had a competitive advantage and larger survival co-efficient which enabled them to reproduce more successfully over the generations. Thus … totemism was indispensable in liberating humans from the hazards of primeval existence, enabling them to join together as sisters and brothers in social life and labor. (39)

The beginnings of 'marriage'

The preceding constitutes merely an introduction to and the conceptual basis for Reed's highly detailed analysis of the process of evolution of our earliest ancestors, during which, Reed demonstrates, the role of women was decisive. We'll focus now, however, on her description of the evolution of "marriage," to which she devotes a whole section of her book, with the title "The Beginnings of Marriage":

> The first step toward marriage was the cross-cousin intermating alliance between two communities. This was not yet marriage since the pair did not change residence or live together under one roof. The man remained a member of his clan and phratry [a group of linked clans comprising one side or moiety of a tribe], the woman of hers. The men of both sides received rights of passage into the territory of the other side to peacefully seek their mates. (273)

Reed argues that the widely reported ceremony which anthropologists have always assumed to be a ritual initiating boys into manhood, a celebration of male puberty, had a very different meaning in the early stages of hominin society:

> The rite of passage called "initiation," … did not originally mark the passage of a youth from childhood to adulthood. It commemorated the passage of a community of "animals" into humans who, as humans, could no longer be killed or eaten. (287)

She further explains:

> Rights of passage [to territories inhabited by other hominin bands] were essential not simply in the quest for food but also in the search for mates who, under the law of exogamy [limiting sexual partners to people outside one's own band or clan], were to be found in alien territory. Thus initiation was in effect a "matrimonial passport" giving the

"marked" men access to one another's territory. ... The various incisions and other marks made on the bodies of the young men during initiation ... served as visible evidence of the youth's new status as an initiated man with the right to enter the territory of his cross-cousins. (291)

Noting that youthful sexual exploration in matrilineal society was unrestricted, Reed comments:

Initiation, therefore, was not designed to initiate the young man into the mysteries of sex. Rather, it was designed to instruct him as to his proper social behavior in the community of his future wife. (299)

And further along:

In the earliest stage of matrimony the husband was little more than a visitor to his wife's community. He did not start out by occupying a separate house or hut with his wife; he was given accommodations in the male clubhouse reserved for strangers and visiting husbands. There under the surveillance of his wife's male kin he slept and took his meals. (304)

The economic origins of 'marriage'

A new stage in marital relations came about with the introduction of gift exchange:

With the development of the gift-giving institution and the increasing breakdown of the hereditary enmity between the intermarrying sides, the mothers' brothers took over the functions of go-betweens for their sisters' daughters and young suitors. Individual pair-matrimony developed on the basis of the community gift-interchange system, which was as much an expression of fraternal relations between the men of the two sides as it was of matrimony. ... The act of interchanging gifts with these former strangers was their assurance that fraternal relations had superseded enmity. (306-307)

But still:

> To pass from ... a liaison to the more substantial union of
> marriage it was necessary for the young woman to invite
> the young man to her mother's house. ... Before a man
> could be promoted from the status of lover to husband he
> must be accepted, that is, "adopted," by his mother-in-law.
> (310-311)

Reed cites a passage from Ruth Benedict's *Patterns of Culture* on the requirements for a successful "adoption":

> From this time forward the young man has to reckon with
> the village of his wife. Its first demand is upon his labor.
> Immediately his mother-in-law gives him a digging-stick
> with the command, "Now, work!" (Benedict 1959: 124)

From gardening, observes Reed:

> [I]t was a short step toward the care and domestication of
> farm animals, and these were the two elements required for
> a higher economy. Thus marriage developed side by side
> with the development of husbandry, a new occupation of
> men which more and more displaced their former occupa-
> tion of hunting. ... Marriage from its inception did not
> hinge upon the sexual relations between a man and a
> woman; it was centered entirely on economic and social
> relations. (313)

Reed has much more to say about prehistoric marriage and prehistoric society in general. But for our purposes we've already reached her most important conclusion: the economic origins of the institution of marriage. In the next chapter, we'll attempt to summarize the somewhat differ-ent, but equally evolutionary and materialist scenario that Marxist anthropologist Chris Knight has constructed in his provocative book, *Blood Relations.*

CHAPTER 14

Domesticating the hunters — Knight's hypothesis

British anthropologist Chris Knight joined a host of militant workers in capitalist society who have lost their jobs for standing up to "the boss." We touched on his acts of political defiance against the imperialist ruling class — which temporarily cost him his livelihood as a professor — in Chapter 12. In this chapter, we'll summarize his radical view of the transformation of hominins into modern humans.

Knight distinguishes himself as an exceptionally capable anthropological theoretician in several ways. Very importantly, he has a good understanding of the science of Marxism and of the historic discoveries of Lewis Henry Morgan, Frederick Engels and Karl Marx in the study of human evolution. In addition, he is an exceptionally well-informed and fair-minded combatant in the ideological class struggle that has unfolded during the last century and a half over the course that anthropological work should follow. Third, his familiarity with the work and writings of other anthropologists is formidable.

At the center of Knight's hypothesis is the development of solidarity uniting the female members of the matrilineal band. In **Blood Relations**, he captures in a single paragraph what follows from this concept:

> In principle, it would only have needed two females — perhaps sisters, perhaps mother and daughter — to have set

in train the movement towards culture as an unstoppable force. If these two always backed each other up, always acted in concert, synchronised their menstrual cycles and were able to motivate two or more males to hunt for them by making sex dependent on it, then they might have been so much more successful in securing meat than other females in the population for their strategy to act as an attractive model, and for any genetic characteristics facilitating such solidarity to spread through the population. (294-295)

'Menstrual synchrony' as a vehicle for female solidarity

First of all, it is important to note Knight's emphasis on "menstrual synchrony":

> Since the 1970s, medical science has begun to acknowledge what countless women must already have known for generations — that when women who are friends associate closely with one another, their cycles begin to synchronise. (212-213)

Knight's use of this phenomenon is superficially similar to that of sociobiologist Paul Turke and his collaborators, who view menstrual synchrony, along with "concealed ovulation" and "continuous but discriminating sexual receptivity" as key to their theory of how human males came to distinguish themselves from their male primate relatives as much better providers. (Turke 1984: 33-44)

Knight is able to distinguish his hypothesis from that of Turke et al. on several grounds:

> Turke's theory rests on no palaeontological or other direct evidence for reproductive synchrony in hominid evolution. The hypothesis is not buttressed with findings from archaeology or from the study of contemporary hunter-gatherers. (219)

It is impossible here even to summarize the mountain of direct evidence and findings that Knight is able to draw on in *Blood Relations* to make demonstrably credible his theory. To offer just one example, though, his use of both region-specific and global climatological data to contextualize and date the process leading to the "human cultural revolution" that he envisions is impressively precise.

Innovation based on climatic stress

Knight writes:

> We will see that everywhere, the decisive events [producing his hypothesized cultural revolution] were associated with periods of combined dryness and cold. (277-278)

He presents evidence that the locational preference of the pre-revolutionary hominins, both in Africa and as they spread out into Eurasia and Australia, was for shoreline areas bordering rivers, lakes and oceans. But dramatic climatic changes, both in Africa and elsewhere, that forced them away from shorelines and into what Knight calls "the hinterlands" were the basis for cultural leaps:

> [A] sophisticated blade-making technology ... dated to about 70,000 BP [years before the present] ... coincides with the onset of a glacial period and worldwide regression of sea levels. ... It was evidently this deterioration which triggered the cultural advance. ... Then at about 40,000 BP came the next major technological advance. ... Again, cold weather had something to do with it. (278)

For Knight, the most important of these climatic shifts was the Last Glacial Maximum, a period of intense global cold between about 26,000 and 19,000 years ago. He writes:

> Despite their tropical origins, modern humans with their warm clothes, semi-permanent dwellings and well-controlled domestic fires embraced the snowswept plains and tundra of ice age Eurasia as if such spaces had been made for them. We must conclude that females in these regions were guaranteeing their subsistence requirements by relating to males in a wholly new way. (279)

The 'sex strike'

And what was that "wholly new way"? To get the male hunters to consistently supply meat to the band or clan, the women established what Knight terms "the sex strike," a menstrually coordinated, periodic refusal by women to have sex with the hunters until the hunters brought back meat to be shared by all. Again, it's not possible to detail here Knight's multifaceted support for this hypothesis. But before we turn to his comments on the institution of "marriage," one crucial byproduct of the sex strike begs for mention.

> A central argument of this book is that … such collective control over sex lies at the root of all sexual "morality." … The "moral" hunter-gatherer woman is the one who keeps in step with her sisters, her kin and/or her gender group, on occasion refusing sex unless or until the male(s) in her life can be induced to behave acceptably, for example by providing meat. … Only one logical thread, carried through to its conclusion, leads us towards central-place foraging, a home base, sexual morality and a genuinely human lifestyle [i.e., the solidarity of women!]. The other thread is a competitive, primate-style "prostitution" pathway [meat for sex on an individual, strikebreaking basis], leading social life in wholly noncultural directions. (188-189)

Based on Knight's hypothesis, the solidarity of the women's sex strike would have made male competition for women a waste of time and would have created the human level of sociality among primordial foragers, fishers and hunters that was envisioned by Frederick Engels in *Origin*:

> Mutual toleration among the adult males, freedom from jealousy, was the first condition for the formation of those larger, permanent groups in which alone animals could become men. (Engels 1972: 100)

Knight counterposes his view of social/sexual relations between the females and males of early human social groups to that of French anthropologist and ethnologist Claude Lévi-Strauss. Knight's view is developed carefully and in great detail, so we'll need to quote him at some length:

> Lévi-Strauss' "exchange of women" model, resting as it does on the absolute primacy of marriage, produces some serious theoretical problems. It precludes female solidarity and fails to explain the patterns actually found in traditionally organised — particularly hunter–gatherer — cultures.
>
> Culture's "initial situation" cannot be dogmatically asserted, but we can be fairly certain that it bore little relation to Lévi-Strauss' picture of women as ever-available, passive pawns in the political schemes of men. It would seem more likely that women, in the course of cultural origins, could give themselves sexually because they had something to give — their bodies were not completely owned or spoken for by the other sex in advance.
>
> Viewing the same feature in the context of the development of hunting and gathering, we may take it that although women did not usually hunt, they could use a measure of control over their own sexual availability to induce men to hunt for them. An implication is that women (supported by their kin) had the capacity to withdraw themselves sexually. In effect — like some female primates but in much more conscious and organised ways — they could go "on strike."

The origin of sexual morality

> Naturally, this did not imply that women did not enjoy sex or that sex seldom happened. It simply means that when sex occurred, it took place as a release from the basic cultural constraints — not in obedience to them. In this sense, no matter how joyfully celebrated and woven into the meanings and symbols of all cultural life, sexual gratification from culture's very beginnings has been

delayed, sublimated and harnessed to economic and other ends, its actual consummation always taking place beyond, behind and in a sense, "in spite of" culture. The bonding involved in love-making, as something tending to undermine wider forms of solidarity, has always been for the public cultural domain something of an embarrassment. …

Of course, there is all the difference in the world between sexually relaxed cultures and more repressive ones in these respects, but in no human social context are people simply uninhibited or unembarrassed in public in the manner of monkeys and apes. In any event, the prioritising of sex has never been allowed to last for long or to threaten society's fundamental economic goals. (151-152)

So we can see, from Evelyn Reed's perspective, which was summarized in Chapter 13, as well as in Chris Knight's analysis here, that from the very beginning of human culture and essential to the first new organizational form of Homo sapiens, economic relations between the sexes played a decisive role. In fact, none of the material that has been reviewed up to this point in the present work gives any reason to believe that the "traditional marriage" form described by anti-evolutionary anthropologist Bronislaw Malinowski in Chapter 1 existed in the millennia previous to what has come to be called "the Agricultural Revolution."

Up to now, our focus has been on the earliest forms of heterosexual relations among hominins and early humans. The ideas presented are of necessity speculative, but are bolstered by a wealth of zoological, archeological, climatological, anthropological, ethnological and other scientific data and, above all, a consistent materialist and evolutionary viewpoint. In the next chapter, we'll review some evidence of same-sex marriage among primordial humans.

CHAPTER 15

Same-sex marriage in pre-class societies

Although the truly nightmarish conditions in the U.S. for lesbian, gay, bisexual, transgender, queer and two-spirit people that existed prior to the Stonewall Rebellion and the modern movement for equal rights and liberation have abated somewhat, the struggle is far from over. Equal rights under bourgeois law are being won through the unrelenting pressure of out-and-proud activists and the refusal of LGBTQ2S people in general to any longer maintain the centuries' long tradition of shame, secrecy and silence.

But being out, especially if you are a transgender person of color, can still mean sudden death or, if you defend yourself like CeCe McDonald did in Minneapolis in 2011, arrest and imprisonment. Full liberation will not be possible until there is a fundamental social transformation — specifically, an end to the rule of capitalism, the decadent, global economic system whose continued existence rests on the perpetuation of racism, sexism, homophobia, genderphobia and all the other weapons it uses to divide and undermine the potential solidarity and political power of workers and oppressed people.

Important scholarly inroads in anthropological and queer studies literature have been and continue to be made concerning the existence of homosexuality and alternate gender expression among the many cultures and historical periods of the world's peoples, but it still requires resolute persistence and digging to find anthropological documentation for prehistoric same-sex marriage. What we're looking for at this point in the present effort are nontransitory same-sex relationships occurring in foraging and hunting groups.

Transgenderal same-sex 'marriage'

In *Queer Science*, author Simon LeVay writes:

> Homosexual relationships fall into a number of different patterns. Among these patterns, three seem to recur widely in different cultures: I will refer to them as transgenderal, age disparate, and companionate relationships. Transgenderal homosexual relationships are those in which one of the two individuals is markedly cross-gendered, while the other is more or less conventional for his or her own sex. In many traditional Native American cultures, for example, there were individuals, known to anthropologists as berdaches (male) or amazons (female), who cross-dressed and took on some of the social roles and attributes of the other sex. (They are sometimes referred to as "two-spirit people.") Berdaches and amazons often married more conventional individuals of the same sex as themselves. (58)

Queer Science has a publication date of 1996. Like Walter Williams in his book *The Spirit and the Flesh*, published eight years earlier, LeVay uses the words "berdache" and "amazon" when referring to Indigenous people, male bodied and female bodied respectively, of mixed or nonbinary gender. In the collection of essays titled *Two-Spirit People* (with a publication date of 1997), the editors, Sue-Ellen Jacobs, Wesley Thomas and Sabine Lang, write:

Two-spirit is the term that all but one of the contributors to this book have agreed to use — for the time being — when writing about those who have previously been termed "berdache" [sic] by anthropologists, historians, sexologists, sociologists, psychologists, and other writers on the subject of sexuality and gender. ...

"Berdache" is now considered to be an inappropriate and insulting term by a number of Native Americans as well as by anthropologists. (the authors' [sic]; 2-3)

And regarding the term "amazon," Jacobs comments on its usage in her ***Two-Spirit People*** essay "Is the 'Berdache' a Phantom in Western Imagination?":

From the perspective of a feminist lesbian, I question why two Anglo female anthropologists ... have used Walter Williams's chapter from ***The Spirit and the Flesh*** (which designates American Indian lesbians, manly-hearted women, and warrior women as "amazons") in an introductory textbook for cross-cultural studies of women. Why did they not use Native American Indian women's own terms for themselves ... ? If Native American women call themselves "lesbian," "dyke," or a multitude of native terms, why should one privilege Williams's use of the term amazon? Is it because the white male voice (whether gay or straight) is assumed to have authority in all scholarly and other matters? Where are Native American women's voices in anthropological writing on this subject? (30-31)

We will return to the topic of "two spirit" in Chapter 30 with a comprehensive statement on the subject by Native activist M. Tiahui.

Midnight Sun is an Anishnawbe Indian lesbian feminist. She has a degree in anthropology/women's studies and, at the time that her essay, "Sex/Gender Systems in Native North America," was published in ***Living the Spirit: A Gay American Indian Anthology*** (Roscoe 1988), she was in training to become a carpenter. Of the three North American tribes she discusses in this essay, only the section on the Mojave people includes material on their homosexual marriage customs. Fortunately, however, she covers Mojave same-sex marriage among women as well as among men. These marriages fall under LeVay's transgenderal category.

Because the larger purpose of Sun's essay is to show the relationship between sex/gender systems and the mode of production or subsistence patterns in three tribal group-ings, she includes basic social and economic information:

> The Mojave are a southwestern American tribe. ... In the late seventeenth century they numbered three thousand and subsisted on small-scale agriculture, supplemented by gathering, hunting and fishing. ... This subsistence strategy, combined with Mojave kinship, marriage, and residence patterns, allowed for relatively egalitarian male-female relations. (36)

The tribe included:

> [H]omosexual and lesbian cross-dressers termed "alyha" (male) and "hwame" (female). Not all homosexual or lesbian behavior entailed assumption of the "alyha" or "hwame" roles, however. Those who were involved in marital or sexual relationships with "alyha" or "hwame," for example, retained the gender identity associated with their biological sex. In other words, Mojave cross-gender categories were distinct from their categories of man and woman. (37)

> "Alyhas" and "hwames" not only adopted the character-istics of the other gender — they fictively conformed to the biological sex characteristics of their assumed genders. For instance, it was reported that when an "alyha" found a potential husband, he imitated menstruation by scratching his legs until they bled. ... "Hwames" found wives at dances and through visiting. ... The Mojave believed that

> intercourse with a pregnant woman could change the
> paternity of a child, so if a "hwame" seduced a pregnant
> woman, "he" was entitled to claim paternity and take care
> of the infant. … The fact that cross-gender individuals were
> often shamans or married to shamans or chiefs suggests
> not only cultural acceptance, but an association with status
> and prestige, as well. This may be due to their value in
> production, because they could combine elements of both
> masculine and feminine economic spheres. (38-39)

The Mojave report, while informative, involves a culture where agricultural production was already part of the economic basis. For a more thoroughly hunting and gathering culture, we turn to a passage written in the latter part of the 16th century and reprinted in *The Spirit and the Flesh*. Portuguese explorer Pedro de Magalhães de Gandavo's report on the Tupinamba Indians of northeastern Brazil included the following observation:

> There are some Indian women who … have no commerce
> with men in any manner. … They give up all the duties of
> women and imitate men, and follow men's pursuits as if
> they were not women. They wear the hair cut in the same
> way as the men, and go to war with bows and arrows and
> pursue game, always in company with men; each has a
> woman to serve her, to whom she says she is married,
> and they treat each other and speak with each other as
> man and wife. (233)

Age-disparate same-sex 'marriage'

David Greenberg's *The Construction of Homosexuality* offers some examples of what might be called age-disparate same-sex marriages in a summary distilled from a number of anthropological studies of New Guinea foraging, hunting and early agricultural societies:

> Transgenerational homosexual relations have been
> studied most thoroughly in New Guinea and parts of
> island Melanesia. … After leaving his mother's hut at age
> twelve or thirteen to take up residence in the men's house,
> a Marind-Anim boy enters into a homosexual relationship
> with his mother's brother, who belongs to a different
> lineage from his own. The relationship endures for
> roughly seven years. …
>
> An Etoro boy's career in homosexuality starts around
> age ten, when he acquires an older partner, ideally his
> sister's husband or fiancé. … The relationship continues
> until the boy develops a full beard in his early to mid-
> twenties. At this point, the now-mature young man
> becomes the older partner of another prepubescent boy,
> ordinarily his wife's or fiancé's younger brother. (27-28)

While these sexual bondings are less than lifelong, they
do suggest, at a minimum, serial homosexual monogamy,
paralleling the descriptions of heterosexual pairing marriages among foraging and hunting peoples.

We find reference to age-disparate same-sex marriage
among women in an essay by John Mburu, titled "Awakenings: Dreams and Delusions of an Incipient Lesbian and
Gay Movement in Kenya." In this work, which appears in
the book *Different Rainbows*, Mburu writes:

> The Nandi of Kenya and Lovedu of South Africa had tradi-
> tions of woman-woman marriage, widespread throughout
> Africa. The practice involved a widowed elderly woman
> taking a younger wife, who helped with household chores
> and bore children as a surrogate for the older woman.
> While a controversy exists as to whether these relationships
> were sexual, among the Azande, women formed lesbian
> relationships amongst themselves that were kept secret
> from their husbands. … Similar relationships were also
> fairly common among the Nupe and Hausa of West Africa.
> (Drucker 2000: 181)

Mburu doesn't address the mode of production of the tribal groupings he names, but material in *Boy-Wives and Female Husbands: Studies in African Homosexualities* suggests that at the time they were observed, these groups were already experiencing the beginnings of economic inequality based on farming. (Murray and Roscoe 1998)

Companionate same-sex 'marriage'

In the groundbreaking work, *Gay American History*, Jonathan Katz includes passages from the writing of Joseph François Lafitau chronicling his experiences as a Jesuit missionary in French Canada between 1711 and 1717. Although veiled in euphemism and obscurantism, his words suggest the existence of LeVay's "companionate relationships" among Native American men, at least some of whom belonged to foraging and hunting groups:

> The … special friendships among young men, which are instituted in almost the same manner from one end of America to the other, are one of the most interesting sides of their customs. … These bonds of friendship … admit of no suspicion of apparent vice, albeit there is, or may be, real vice. They are highly ancient in their origin, highly marked in the constancy of their practice, consecrated, if I dare say as much, in the union they create, whose bonds are as close as those of blood and nature. … The parents are the first to encourage them and to respect their rights. (289)

While there may, indeed, be examples of companionate relationships qualifying as "same-sex marriages" among foraging and hunting women, our very cursory search found no clear examples. Given the tendency of many anthropological reports to focus mainly on men and often ignore, minimize or distort the roles of women, this shouldn't be surprising.

But several other factors are involved. Female members of foraging and hunting groups are not likely to share with male investigators information on their sexual activities or relationships. In fact, after initial, unpleasant contact with Christian missionaries or other representatives of patriarchal society, neither women nor men of foraging and hunting societies are likely to speak openly about matters which they already know these outsiders disapprove of or view with disdain. Finally, though, we can be sure that the matrilineal clan form of social organization provided ample opportunities for long-term, companionate relationships between women.

While the word "marriage" may or may not be used to characterize transgenderal, age disparate and companionate homosexual relationships among foraging and hunting peoples, the reports we've reviewed are strong evidence that such relationships existed as a part of early human societies, were much more than promiscuous, transient "couplings," and, most importantly, benefited from the general acceptance and benign approval of their heterosexually oriented kin. We need to learn from our ancestors!

The following chapters will describe a fundamental transformation in human social relations paralleling the adoption of agricultural production, a transformation that included disastrous implications for women, homosexual relations, gender nonconformity and the institution of "marriage."

CHAPTER 16

An overview of the 'Agricultural Revolution'

The word "revolution" conjures up the image of a quick, qualitative, monumental and tumultuous change. The Neolithic or so-called Agricultural Revolution did, in fact, bring about a qualitative and monumental transformation of human social/sexual relations, but it was in no sense quick, although it must have included tumultuous episodes. Its commencement is usually dated to the end of the last Ice Age, about 11,600 years ago.

This transition is summarized in *The Human Past* edited by Chris Scarre. On page 182, Scarre writes:

> Already during the final stages of the last Ice Age, certain groups of hunters and gatherers had begun to exploit their environment in a new way, moving beyond simple collecting to the intentional management of selected plant species. Thus began the process of domestication and cultivation that has transformed the world. Spreading inexorably from its origins in a number of separate regions, the shift from food collection to food production dramatically increased the human carrying capacity of the planet. In the process, the environment was transformed, as modest clearings gave way to fields, and forests were felled to provide farmland for ever-increasing human numbers.

Scarre suggests at least seven areas of the planet where agriculture probably developed independently: the New

Guinea highlands, the Yanzi and Yellow River basins, the so-called Fertile Crescent, Sub-Saharan Africa, Amazonia, Central Mexico and Eastern North America.

Agriculture based on accumulated knowledge of matriarchal clans

It's important to note, however, the roots of this movement toward a new mode of food acquisition. It's scarcely an arguable point that the humans who used foraging, fishing and hunting for food sustenance would have had profound knowledge and understanding of the natural world. Their very survival would have depended on that knowledge. Anthropologists have been astounded at the depth of knowledge that the seafaring peoples of the Pacific islands had of the night sky, a knowledge of the positions and movement of the stars and planets that guaranteed the seafarers safe passage from island to island without the use of compasses or sextants. Similarly, the foraging and hunting peoples of the African plains understood in detail the behavior patterns of the animals they depended on for part of their diet and otherwise shared their environment with. And the tribal women of the Amazonian rain forest knew the useful characteristics of thousands of plants.

Anthropological evidence makes it clear that women were not passive onlookers of the movement to agricultural production. As they had previously been the main foragers, their knowledge of plants led them to early experiments in selective cultivation. As keepers of the fire, they were the innovators, first, of the use of cooking stones and later of pottery, for preparing, heating and preserving food and for food storage. They also had an important role in the capture and domestication of small animals.

On the other hand, the men's hunting-based familiarity with large animals gave them the edge in the domestication and management of herds of cattle and draft animals that could be trained to pull plows over large expanses of cropland. Like pairing marriages, which developed a social bond outside of matrilineal kinship, intensive farming, managed by men but aided by their wives and children, had the long-term effect of fragmenting the matrilineal solidarity of clan and tribal society.

The increase in food yield from farming combined with new storage techniques meant periodic surpluses, important for the cold months in temperate zones, but also introducing a new social issue: Who would have control of the surplus and decide how it should be disposed of?

A complex, dispersed, nonuniform process

In *Origin*, Frederick Engels began his discussion of the Agricultural Revolution with the following words:

> Thus far we have been able to follow a general line of development applicable to all peoples at a given period without distinction of place. With the beginning of barbarism [the unfortunate term that early anthropologists used to describe the transition from foraging and hunting to agriculture], however, we have reached a stage when the difference in the natural endowments of the two hemispheres of the earth comes into play. … Owing to these differences in natural conditions, the population of each hemisphere now goes on its own way, and different landmarks divide the particular stages in each of the two cases. (89-90)

Engels noted that there are important differences in what animal species were available for domestication and which cultivable cereals were available in the Eastern and Western hemispheres, and this makes global generalizations about the introduction of agriculture difficult. In areas where crop cultivation was not feasible because of poor climatic or soil conditions, nomadic or semi-nomadic patterns based on hunting and/or fishing continued. Under these conditions, the domestication and breeding of herds was the primary form of surplus accumulation.

Resistance to agricultural production

A caveat needs to be added to the obvious advantage of plant cultivation and animal breeding in increasing the available supply of food, however. Ethnologists who have done field studies of the two distinct modes of food production have noted that, from a nutritional point of view, foraging and hunting often result in a more varied and more nutritious diet, and from a work output point of view, foraging and hunting is less labor intensive and less time consuming.

So the strong resistance to the introduction of farming that has been reported for some contemporary foraging and hunting groups who are able to sustain themselves with only a few hours of foraging each week and occasional hunting successes is suggestive of similar misgivings by prehistoric groups living in naturally bountiful circumstances.

Anthropologist Richard Lee's paper, "What Hunters Do for a Living," appears in the misnamed book, *Man the Hunter*, a collection of anthropological reports whose contents actually contain abundant evidence of the predominant importance of women's activities over those of hunting. Lee's paper focuses on the !Kung Bushmen of Botswana. He writes:

A diet based on mongongo nuts is in fact more reliable than one based on cultivated foods, and it is not surprising, therefore, that when a Bushman was asked why he hadn't taken to agriculture, he replied, "Why should we plant, when there are so many mongongo nuts in the world?" (Lee and DeVore 1968: 33)

Surplus and social inequality

The probable key to what ultimately motivated the transition to production based on agriculture most likely lies in the resulting surplus beyond the group's immediate needs. With the technological innovation that preservation and storage techniques represented, the surplus was a source of potential economic and political power previously unknown. And as patrilineal, patrilocal families replaced matrilineal clans, that surplus brought a new, higher economic, social and political status to men. Replacing the matrilineal clan and the pairing marriage was an increasingly socially fragmented society with a male-dominated political structure based on male control of the agricultural surplus: the herds of cattle and stores of grain.

Paleolithic c. 20,000 B.C., found in France. Female figurines have been uncovered in sites all around the world dating to a time during the early development of agriculture. Many have sagging breasts and bellies suggesting older women.

What was lost included the communality and social equality of women and men; the wise guidance of the councils of older women; the humane, communal ethics that ensured the well-being of all the members of the clan; the collective care that was of such great benefit to the children and the elders; and the relaxed, relatively unrestricted enjoyment of exogamous sex.

We've already had a glimpse, in the concluding words of Evelyn Reed at the end of Chapter 13, of the likely process through which matrilineal society in general and pairing marriage in particular were qualitatively transformed. In this chapter, we've outlined the economic basis of this monumental change: the introduction of agricultural production. In the next chapter, we'll take up this historic, actually still prehistoric, transformation in greater detail, focusing especially on the political implications for "marriage" of what Marxists call "the overthrow of mother right."

This image, given the name "Running Horned Woman," appears on a rock dated to approximately 6,000 to 4,000 B.C.E. It was found in a canyon in the Algerian section of the Sahara Desert.

Fine fringes fall from the knees, the belt and the outstretched arms. From either side of the head and above two horns is a dotted area resembling a cloud of grain falling from a wheat field.

CHAPTER 17

For women, the Agricultural Revolution was a counterrevolution

How, in the view of 19th-century anthropologist Lewis Henry Morgan, did early human society based on mother right, or matrilineality and matrilocality, become patrilineal and patriarchal?

For his explanation in *Ancient Society,* Morgan drew on his knowledge of the evolution that resulted in Grecian and Latin patriarchal clans:

> [Matrilineal clans] possessed the following among other characteristics: 1. Marriage in the gens [clan] was prohibited; thus placing children in a different gens from that of their reputed father. 2. Property and the office of chief were hereditary in the gens; thus excluding children from inheriting the property or succeeding to the office of their reputed father. This state of things would continue until a motive arose sufficiently general and commanding to establish the injustice of this exclusion in the face of their changed condition.
>
> The natural remedy was a change of descent from the female to the male. All that was needed to effect this change was an adequate motive. After domestic animals began to be reared in flocks and herds, becoming thereby a source of subsistence as well as objects of individual property, and after tillage had led to the ownership of

houses and lands in severalty [property owned by individual right, not held in common], an antagonism would be certain to arise against the prevailing form of gentile inheritance, because it excluded the owner's children, whose paternity was becoming more assured, and gave his property to his gentile kindred.

A contest for a new rule of inheritance, shared in by fathers and their children, would furnish a motive sufficiently powerful to effect the change. With property accumulating in masses and assuming permanent forms, and with an increased proportion of it held by individual ownership, descent in the female line was certain of overthrow, and the substitution of the male line assured. (345-346)

Monogamous marriage, material surplus and private property

Along with a change in the line of descent, a new form of marriage emerged in the realm of social/sexual relations. Frederick Engels writes in *Origin*:

> [Monogamous marriage] is based on the supremacy of the man, the express purpose being to produce children of undisputed paternity; such paternity is demanded because these children are later to come into their father's property as his natural heirs. It is distinguished from pairing marriage by the much greater strength of the marriage tie, which can no longer be dissolved at either partner's wish. As a rule, it is now only the man who can dissolve it and put away his wife. (125)

Engels continues:

> [Monogamous marriage] was not in any way the fruit of individual sex love, with which it had nothing whatever to do. … It was the first form of the family to be based not on natural but on economic conditions — on the victory of private property over primitive, natural communal property.

… When monogamous marriage first makes its appearance in history, it is not as the reconciliation of man and woman, still less as the highest form of such a reconciliation.

Quite the contrary, monogamous marriage comes on the scene as the subjugation of the one sex by the other; it announces a struggle between the sexes unknown throughout the whole previous prehistoric period. In an old unpublished manuscript written by Marx and myself in 1846, I find the words: "The first division of labor is that between man and woman for the propagation of children." And today I can add: The first class opposition that appears in history coincides with the development of the antagonism between man and woman in monogamous marriage, and the first class oppression coincides with that of the female sex by the male. (128-129)

Further along in *Origin*, Engels elaborates on the ramifications of the sexual division of labor following the introduction of material surplus:

The "savage" warrior and hunter had been content to take second place in the house, after the woman; the "gentler" shepherd, in the arrogance of his wealth, pushed himself forward into the first place and the woman down into the second. … The division of labor within the family had regulated the division of property between the man and the woman. That division of labor had remained the same; and

Subjects bringing gifts to the King in Persepolis, the ceremonial capital of the Achaemenid Empire, c. 500 B.C. (Present day Iran)

yet it now turned the previous domestic relation upside down simply because the division of labor outside the family had changed. (221)

Engels is referring, of course, to the man's effective possession and control of the agricultural surplus represented by the animal herds and stores of grain.

The sexual counterrevolution

Engels notes:

Together with slavery and private wealth, [monogamous marriage] opens the period that has lasted until today in which every step forward is also relatively a step backward, in which prosperity and development for some is won through the misery and frustration of others. (129)

What was the nature of this "misery and frustration"? Engels discusses at length how the imposition of monogamy meant a serious restriction on women's sexual rights. For men, he observes, it has been a frequently ignored or disregarded obstacle. But much more than women's sexual rights was lost:

The overthrow of mother right was the "world historic defeat of the female sex." The man took command in the home also; the woman was degraded and reduced to servitude; she became the slave of his lust and a mere instrument for the production of children. (120-121)

The bitter truth described by these words has almost global confirmation in the recorded histories of women's lives on every populated continent.

In the booklet *Feminism and Marxism*, Dorothy Ballan provided important ideological outreach to the burgeoning U.S. women's movement of some fifty years ago when she wrote:

The origin of the word "family" meant slave, and the family included a man, his wife, children and slaves. The women were acquired into this economic unit for the purpose of procreating heirs to whom to bequeath private property — and as such, the family served the interests of the possessing class.

This was the real origin of the family. When social production became transformed into private production, the nature of the family changed from a socially cooperative foundation as it existed under the matriarchy to the private foundations of the patriarchy. ... The conversion of social property to private property eventually meant even the conversion of humans to private ownership.

For primitive women, childbearing not only provided a greater impetus for her to participate in social production, but was virtually a form of social production itself. The husband had no authority over her, and she was never dependent upon him economically or materially.

This became transformed into its opposite, with marriage and childbearing isolating and insulating women from social production, making her totally dependent on her husband, and reducing her to the role of procreation for inheritance, and to the role of servant for [her] husband. (16)

As we stressed at the beginning of Chapter 16, the so-called Agricultural Revolution, with the accompanying transition to patriarchal, class-divided society and "monogamous" marriage for the woman, was neither a quick nor a simple change. In the following several chapters we will only be able to touch on some general aspects of this complex and prolonged counterrevolution of the social/sexual relations between men and women, a transformation based on the introduction of private property.

The appearance of writing coincided with the appearance of great private wealth. This example of early writing on a clay tablet dates to 3100-3000 B.C.E. and was found in what is now southern Iraq. It records the allocation of beer as rations to a group of Mesopotamian workers. The holders of great wealth in the early city-states of the Middle East, mostly powerful political and religious figures, needed written records to keep track of their booty.

CHAPTER 18

From matrilineal clan to patriarchy – polygyny in transitional societies

The transition to sedentary life and agricultural production was a process carried out in different ways and at different times in different parts of the planet's inhabited areas. Up to this point, we and our more theoretically oriented sources have been drawing inferences from archaeological and anthropological reports. Our objective has been to extrapolate from contemporary scientific reports what social/sexual relations must have been like during the many millennia before people achieved the domestication of animals and cultivation of plants.

While it is still something of a leap from the patterns of life of transitional groups existent during the last few hundred years back to the originators of agriculture 10 or 12 millennia ago, it's less of a leap than that which theorists make in hypothesizing the hominin life patterns of hundreds of thousands of years ago. Therefore, our confidence is strengthened that we can glean from more or less contemporary reports some idea of the processes at work during the transition from the matrilineal clan to patriarchal families whose sustenance was obtained more from farming than from foraging or hunting.

Anthropologists David Schneider and Kathleen Gough co-edited a collection of essays with the title *Matrilineal Kinship* in 1961. The societies they chose for study, however, are more accurately classed as transitional forms, retaining some of the social features of matrilineal hunter-gatherer societies but well on their way to patriarchal dominance based on the adoption of food production techniques characteristic of the Agricultural Revolution.

Schneider writes in the book's "Preface":

> The selection of societies [for the section of the book he edited and contributed to] did provide a wide diversity of types of matrilineal system. Drawing them from four continents minimized the possibility that any constant features discovered might result from diffusion rather than from matrilineal descent. The traditional Navajo and Plateau Tonga societies were examples of loosely structured, acephalous [leaderless] tribes. ... Both rely not only on cultivation but also on herding — unusual for matrilineal peoples. Truk and Trobriand are examples of more tightly structured matrilineal systems with relatively settled cultivation, organized into chiefdoms. The Ashanti were a large, matrilineally organized state, while the Kerala castes were differentiated occupational and social strata within still larger states. (xv)

Even this single paragraph from the "Preface" contains examples of some of the diverse paths taken in the transi-

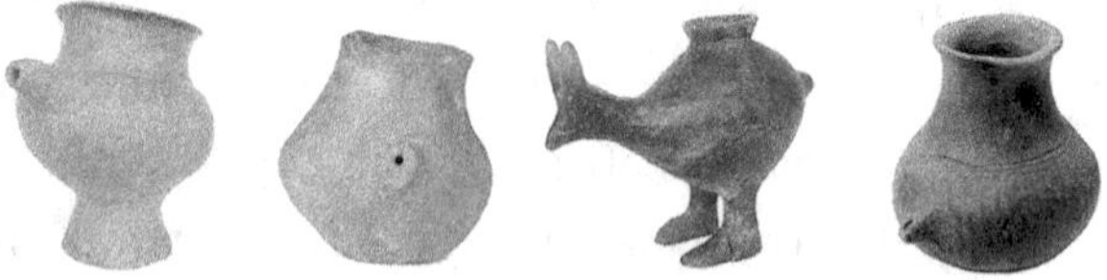

Prehistoric baby bottles dated back more than 7,000 years to the dawn of agriculture.

tion to patriarchy that followed from the adoption of agricultural production.

The social significance of herding — and imperialist intervention!

We think it odd that Schneider characterizes the Navajo and Tonga as "leaderless." In the chapter dealing with the Navajo, we learn that women in this society play a dominant role in the raising of sheep, an important source of material surplus. This, in turn, suggests significant economic and political power on their part, which would later be constrained and distorted, of course, by the genocidal imposition of reservation life. In 1862, the U.S. Congress authorized the creation of Fort Sumner as a strategic outpost for the forced movement of 9,000 Apaches and Navajos into a 40-square-mile reservation.

Judging from the coverage in *Matrilineal Kinship* of the Plateau Tonga of Zambia, it is Tonga men who control the raising of cattle, with resultant significant economic inequality. Like the Navajo, the Tonga suffered from imperialist domination. Under British colonial rule, a system was installed at the beginning of the 20th century taxing Tonga men, effectively forcing on Tonga society a cash-based economic system. It is perhaps the imperialist subjugation of the Navajo and the Plateau Tonga that suggests to Schneider that they are "leaderless."

Returning to Schneider's preliminary assessment that we quoted above, we note that none of the societies there dealt with base themselves on foraging and hunting. And they all appear to be sedentary rather than nomadic. A reasonable conclusion is that what exists of matrilineality in these societies represents not much more than a vestige of the full social/sexual equality found in the matrilineal clans of foragers and hunters. How, then, are the nontransient social/ sexual relations between women and men in these societies affected by economies capable of producing significant surplus and no longer governed by communality and sharing?

Polygyny among the Navajo and Tonga

Coverage of Navajo marriage in *Matrilineal Kinship* includes an extended discussion of polygyny. A late 19th-century report indicates that at that time, more than 50 percent of married men had two or more wives. Marriage was exogamous — partners had to be from outside the suitor's clan — and the preference, according to the report, was for two sisters or classificatory sisters — nonblood relations of the same clan and same age range — to marry the same man. A mid-20th century report suggested that "the large, polygynous family is helpful for livestock operations." (120)

Another common pattern was for interclan marriages between two brothers and two sisters or between a brother and sister and a sister and a brother. This pattern would, perhaps, have facilitated interclan alliances even more than single marriages would. Levirate marriages, where the brother of a dead man would replace the dead man as the dead man's widow's new husband, and sororate marriages, where the sister of a dead woman would replace the dead woman as the dead woman's widower's new wife, were also reported among the Navajo at the beginning of the 20th century.

Significant economic inequality among the Navajo is indicated by the range of bride prices. Some casual marriages were effected with no bride price, but wealthy families might release their daughters only upon payment of from one to fifteen horses. This is a far cry from the foraging and hunt-

A wall painting from an Egyptian tomb, 3,500 B.C., illustrating the development of agriculture.

ing customs involving a modest food exchange between the clans of the husband and wife, or a labor commitment on the part of the new husband to the wife's clan.

Polygynous marriages are also a factor among the Plateau Tonga, according to the report in *Matrilineal Kinship*, with 24 percent of married men having more than one wife. One of the important motives for polygyny among the Tonga is "to have the labor of a number of wives and their children to work the man's own field." (61) For the woman, an interesting contradiction arises.

On the one hand, she achieves a certain amount of economic independence:

> Each wife is entitled from the time of marriage to her own hut. When her separate household is established, she becomes entitled to her own kitchen, her own field, and her

own granary. She can be required to work only in her own field and in the separate field of her husband. Neither she nor her children need work in the field of her co-wife. (62)

But on the other hand, with this new "freedom" the female solidarity and communal sharing characteristic of the foraging and hunting matrilineal clan has been lost.

And ominously:

The introduction of ploughing has reinforced the husband's rights over fields and crops. Because the plough and oxen used in the fields are usually his, he claims that he is entitled to all the proceeds over and above that needed for food without regard to whose field produced the crop. If he has also provided the seed, his certainty that he is absolute master of the crop is increased. (71)

CHAPTER 19

Bioarchaeologists tackle the transition from matrilineal clans to patriarchy

Old bones and teeth, and rocks with signs of having been worked on by humans, are the only objects that give voice to our most ancient ancestors. But even zooming through the many millennia of hominin evolution to the dawn of the Agricultural Revolution, we're still dealing with prehistory … no written records! Jane Peterson and the many archaeological colleagues she cites in *Sexual Revolutions: Gender and Labor at the Dawn of Agriculture*, have, through a combination of ingenuity and scientific acumen, been able to determine much about that transitional period, at least as it unfolded in southwest Asia.

Peterson is an expert in the analysis of ancient bones and teeth for markers of occupational stress (MOS). Differential patterns of MOS, she explains, provide insights into differing patterns of labor.

> Studies of trauma, dental wear, arthritis, bone structure, and muscle development have all been used to discuss workload and activity patterns. … When analyzed and interpreted within and between sex categories, MOS can provide information germane to labor divisions within a population. (7)

Especially because she is investigating possibly differing patterns of labor between men and women at the onset of agricultural production, she is careful to note the difficulty with sex and gender terminology:

> I will employ the distinction between "sex" as a biologically determined variable and "gender" as a cultural construct. … Sex generally refers to one of two categories defined on the basis of external genitalia. From the osteological perspective, it refers to an estimation of these two categories based on standard skeletal criteria. … While there is often close correspondence between sex and gender categories, some cultures define additional gender role options. … The occasional use of the terms "gender" or "engendered" acknowledges the possibility that sexual identity is a more complex, less dichotomous, and culturally specific construct. (7)

Archaeologists have devised increasingly precise tests for dating the residue of past human presence and activity. With regard to Peterson's purview in this book, in what she labels the southern Levant (today mostly Zionist occupied Palestine), archaeologists have distinguished five main periods (with some further subdivisions we needn't be concerned with here): the Natufian (12,500 to 10,000 B.P. (before the present)); the Pre-Pottery Neolithic (10,500 to 7,700 B.P.); the Pottery Neolithic (7,700 to 6,200 B.P.); the Chalcolithic (6,200 to 5,500 B.P.); and the Early Bronze 1 (5,500 to 5,000 B.P.).

> The Natufians were semi-sedentary hunter-gatherers who used wild plants intensively and hunted game, primarily gazelle. During the Pre-Pottery Neolithic periods, groups employed domestic plants and animals in sedentary village contexts for the first time. … During the succeeding Pottery Neolithic and Chalcolithic periods, domestic animals became increasingly important. A range of

settlement types reflects a variety of cultural solutions to this new economic base. Some groups lived in sedentary, mixed agricultural settlements, while others seem to have been more mobile, with a greater reliance on domesticated animals and their products. ... During the Early Bronze I, an agropastoral lifestyle, one that relied on domestic plants, herded animals, and animal by-products, emerged. (8-10)

Stress markers point to the exploitation of women

For the challenge of uncovering changes in the sexual division of labor through these periods, Peterson and other bioarchaeologists turn to the analysis of long-bone robusticity, joint modification, trauma, tooth wear and musculoskeletal stress markers (MSM). To laypeople, like the present author, these high technology efforts are little short of amazing, but Peterson is at pains to caution the reader: "It is important to temper our optimism about the potentials of bioarchaeological data with the reality of osteological material sometimes more than 10,000 years old." (10)

Nevertheless, the summary of findings she offers prior to what is a highly technical, book length discussion are, from this writer's point of view, provocative:

> One clear pattern of sexually divided labor occurs during the Natufian, when male participation in hunting appears to be significant. However, I characterize the overall sexual division of labor as weak during the Natufian because, beyond the muscle signatures associated with hunting, males and females often have broadly similar MSM profiles. Even fewer differences in activity and workload were discerned between Neolithic males and females. Neolithic labor patterns are marked by a convergence in MSM profiles, leaving open the question of sexually divided labor. Subsequently, during the Early

Bronze I, activity patterns shift again. Female activity levels increase substantially relative to their male counterparts, and MSM profiles suggest that more pronounced divisions of sexual labor developed during the Early Bronze I period relative to either the Natufian or the Neolithic. (11)

So, labor efforts of men and women in the period before the dawn of the Agricultural Revolution in the southern Levant appear to be at a similar level, with the qualification that the hunting efforts of men were a distinguishing feature. With the diminution of male hunting efforts and the commencement of modest agricultural activities in the Neolithic, the level of labor efforts of men and women showed even stronger equalization. But as the domestication of animals became an important economic factor in the Early Bronze I, the labor efforts of women, in comparison with those of men, "increase[d] substantially."

Peterson is a very cautious scientist. In the concluding chapter, she elaborates a little on her findings for the Early Bronze I period:

> Assuming that health problems were not affecting males differently than females, male activity levels decrease notably compared to females, as measured by a number of indices. Over time, the level and types of activities carried out by females appear to change less dramatically than do those of males. Now, for the first time, I see evidence for a well-established sex-based division of labor. (145)

How to account for this development? Peterson is silent. But a reasonable person familiar with Engels' *Origin* might hazard an explanation based on the overthrow of mother-right: the men's exploitation of the women's labor had commenced!

Finally, it bears comment that Peterson mentions concern about "health problems" among the agriculturalists. Other scientists have speculated on the likelihood of transference of animal diseases to humans once animal domestication necessitated, for the first time, long-term close contact with living animals. This, along with the grueling labor, nutritionally restricted diets and the enslavement of women, highlights the negative side of the Agricultural Revolution.

What a difference 1,000 years makes

Archaeologist and author Brenna Hassett, in her book *Built on Bones: 15,000 Years of Urban Life and Death*, offers a less technically challenging picture of the changing circumstances of human life during the Neolithic:

> What we see in the archaeological record is far more complex than a linear march of one particularly successful idea or genetic group. The constant movement of people and genetic expansions, mixing and admixing, the to-and-fro of waves of humans between Africa, Europe and Asia through the tide pools of the Near East, leaves a strange residue of Neolithic populations and cultures behind. (2017: 84)
>
> The fertility-rise harbinger of our species' enormous swing vote for farming is something we can access, albeit with a great deal of trouble. The evidence of increasing fertility I saw in my work in Central Anatolia, locked into the teeth of children 10,000 years gone, argues for a similarly slow boil at work in the ancient Near East as in the Americas. Occupation at Asikli Höyük lasted at least a millennium, with nearby Çatalhöyük occupied for the millennium that followed. That is an astonishing swath of time to get around to sorting out being a village, and it's entirely possible that the foot-dragging nature of our

march to urban life reflects a real problem: the Neolithic was dangerous. …

My recent collaborative research with Emmy Bocaege of the University of Bordeaux has emphasized the dangers of this transition. Using incredibly fine-grained analysis of tooth growth … she has uncovered a pattern of growth disruption in the teeth of the children of Çatalhöyük showing that they were consistently exposed to episodes of either malnutrition, disease or some other metabolic stress. Compared to the earlier, less firmly Neolithised inhabitants of Asikli, the children of Çatalhöyük appear to have had a harder time of it. They suffered a higher number of incidents that left scars on the dental record of their growth. (87)

At Asikli in particular, there are no signs of the personal goods or gods that might mark out individuals or households with different access to resources, be they material or metaphysical. Large communal storage and communal spaces with traces of a central hearth, ample seating and remains of collective activities like feasting testify to a much more egalitarian mode of existence.

Slowly, however, the communal spaces of the earliest villages get roofed over, and the passage between the personal world and the communal world gets narrower. We see this physical shift in the very nature of buildings themselves, as the great collective communities of the early agricultural experimentalists start to reshape themselves to meet the demands of a growing population. Individual hearths inside individual buildings replace the old ones that sat outside, open to all. Communal storage gives way to individual hoards, the surplus potential of agricultural wealth suddenly something to accumulate and protect. The big public spaces for feasting and rituals that tie the community together shrink, or are slowly elevated out of reach of the commons. We see doorways on temples and

> hidden rooms where the gods are available only for private conversations with a select few. … New sites are founded, this time with walls. (100-101)

This might be a good place to note that Hassett, like a number of other authorities, mischaracterizes the dialectical materialist view of human history (Marx and Engels' viewpoint) as "a linear march of one particularly successful idea or genetic group." Although agriculture was, over much of the planet, ultimately victorious over foraging and hunting, the process was driven, as we hope the facts laid down in this work attest, by dialectics, the interplay and contention of opposing forces — material contradictions!

CHAPTER 20

Social tensions facilitate the transition from matrilineal clans to patriarchy

The foundational contradictions posited by Evelyn Reed and Chris Knight (see Chapters 13 and 14) outline chronologically remote, prehistoric dialectical processes (the interests of the men vs. the interests of the women) in the relations between the sexes that set the stage, first, for the period of matrilineal clans and mother right and, later, for the transition to agriculture and slavery/feudalism.

According to Knight's hypothesis, the male hunters were induced by a women's sex strike to share the product of their kills. Reed's basic argument is that the hominin hunters were induced by the hominin women to give up the practice of cannibalism and become farmers.

There is no necessary conflict between the evolutionary materialist stories of these two pro-Marxist theoreticians. Viewed chronologically, Reed's two-part hypothesis would probably straddle Knight's, with Reed's hypothesis of male hominins overcoming cannibalism preceding Knight's hypothesis of the human female solidarity sex strike, which, in turn, would logically be followed millennia later by the push of the women of the matrilineal clans for the domesticated hunters to become horticulturalists.

Kin-based vs. nonkin-based loyalties

As noted in previous chapters, the pairing marriage characteristic of the matrilineal clans had an exogamous character; pairings were made between clans, with the "husband" visiting or relocating to the woman's clan from his own maternal clan. These moves had the benefit of initiating and building connections between clans, which meant building trust and networks of mutual support. But while the practice had the immediate effect of contributing to interclan alliances and solidarity, its long-term effect contributed to undermining matrilineality and the communal nature of the clan.

Reed writes in *Woman's Evolution*:

> It is the men who are most affected by the conflict between matrilineality and matrimony. The man who leaves his own community for that of his wife has divided interests and loyalties. All his basic rights, responsibilities, and allegiances are with his sisters and other matrikin. This inhibits the fuller development of his ties with his wife and her children. (319-320)

Further along she writes:

> As against the husband-wife pair joined in marriage, there arises what may be called a counter-institution, the sister-brother pair united in matrilineality. ...
> The antagonistic coexistence of sister-brother and husband-wife can be viewed as the harbinger of fundamental changes taking place in the matriarchal structure. (324)

This source of social/sexual tension, resting on a contradiction between kin and nonkin relations, was by itself, however, an insufficient basis for the qualitative transformation in social/sexual relations that was to come. Reed adds another kin/nonkin source of social/sexual tension that developed from the social pattern spelled out in many anthropological reports. She describes how potential "husbands" were accepted into the prospective wife's clan.

Winning the acceptance of the prospective wife's matrikin and, in particular, that of the prospective mother-in-law, involved working for them. Reed writes:

> He becomes a husband when he has passed through the ordeal and is ready to accept the work of husbandry. …
> One meaning of "husband" is "a man who has a wife." But a "husbandman" is a farmer, a tiller of the ground. Thus the husband makes his appearance in history as a gardener working for his wife's kin. (312)

Reed emphasizes the profound political significance of men embracing farming over hunting and how this development occurred in parallel with a new form of social/sexual relations between men and women, something much more akin to what is considered "marriage" in modern society:

> From gardening [horticulture] it was a short step toward the care and domestication of farm animals [full-blown agriculture], and these were the two elements required for a higher economy. Thus marriage developed side by side with the development of husbandry, a new occupation of men which more and more displaced their former occupation of hunting. (312-313)

Eleanor Leacock elucidates the contradiction that results, for a few fortunate farmers, from the employment of diligent husbandry in her "Introduction" to the 1972 edition to *Origin*:

> [T]he accumulation of individual wealth and the separation of society into privileged and non-privileged classes … [results in] [p]rivate estates [which] are built up through the transmission of property within family lines, rather than within the larger kin group, and the family becomes a power against the gens. (47)

The contradictory character of the gift

Another source of social tension originating among the matrilineal clans was a practice whose initial effect, like that of exogamous sexual relations, was to initiate and build networks of trust and mutual support among neighboring clans. This was the custom of gift exchange.

From an evolutionary point of view, gift exchange initially functioned as a largely symbolic extension to the inter-clan level of the intraclan sharing of resources, which was an essential characteristic of communal, matrilineal society. Its importance was examined in detail by Marcel Mauss in his book *The Gift: The Form and Reason for Exchange in Archaic Societies.*

Mauss stresses the collective and symbolic nature of gift giving in what he terms "archaic societies":

> First, it is not individuals but collectivities that impose
> obligations of exchange and contract upon each other. ...
> Moreover, what they exchange is not solely property. ...
> In particular, such exchanges are acts of politeness ...
> in which the passing on of wealth is only one feature of a
> much more general and enduring contract. Finally, these
> total services and counter-services are committed to in a
> somewhat voluntary form by presents and gifts, although
> in the final analysis they are strictly compulsory, on pain of
> private or public warfare. (5)

Summarizing his anthropologically based analysis, Mauss writes:

> Thus, in four important population groups [of foragers
> and hunters] we have discovered ... the archaic form of
> exchange — that of gifts presented and reciprocated.
> Moreover, we have identified the circulation of things in
> these societies with the circulation of rights and persons.

... The number, extent, and importance of these facts justifies fully our conception of a regime that must have been shared by a very large part of humanity during a very long transitional phase, one that, moreover, still subsists among the peoples we have described. (46)

But like exogamy, reciprocal gift giving produced contradictory pressures. The "compulsory" or obligatory nature of the exchange would become problematical when the evolving technology of agricultural food production and food storage began producing surplus beyond immediate needs. The inevitable economic inequality based on factors like differences in productivity that resulted in differential quantities of food surplus was, perhaps, first expressed in the phenomenon of feasting, a widespread practice among early agriculturalists that we'll consider in detail in the next chapter.

CHAPTER 21

Feasting as a patriarchal instrument for deepening social inequality

The dissolution of the matrilineal clan effectively isolated the woman from her mothers, sisters and brothers. She, rather than her husband, became the outsider: first, as a new addition to her husband's patrilineal, patrilocal clan, and later — as growing economic inequality tore asunder all vestiges of clan society — as an agricultural worker and household slave in a patriarchal family unit.

The institution of slavery was unknown in pre-class society. When captives were taken in interclan conflicts, they were either killed or adopted into the victorious clan. Even as the beginnings of political inequality appeared with the rise of tribal chiefdoms, as long as the prevailing mode of production was foraging-hunting, the idea of singling out some special group of people to work solely for the benefit of others was unthinkable.

The development of material surplus and the accompanying economic inequality that it engendered changed all that. In Chapter 18, we described how, with the introduction of agricultural production, polygynous marriages were one important source of additional labor — in the form of multiple wives and their children — that men's enterprises like cattle herding and crop cultivation required. The previous work obligation that the potential husband owed to the woman's clan — a way of winning their approval to the idea of his joining their clan — became something totally different.

Now, the ambitious and fortunate farmer, whose agricultural surplus was a source of economic power, could afford to pay a substantial bride price to his prospective wife's family for what, in addition to having a sex partner, actually constituted access to her labor power, hopefully over her entire adult lifetime. What word should be used to describe this relationship?

Feasting as an innovation of transitional society

Since it was not all farmers, but only the most "ambitious and fortunate" ones, who were able to accumulate the wealth and prestige that constituted the raw material for the first class societies, it would deepen our understanding of this transition to examine one of the social practices that helped to effect this change. This nearly worldwide phenomenon found in transitional societies has recently received detailed consideration by archeologists, ethnographers and anthropologists in a book-length collection of papers titled *Feasts: Archaeological and Ethnographic Perspectives on Food, Politics, and Power.* (Dietler and Hayden 2001)

Co-editors Michael Dietler and Brian Hayden explain their interest in the subject and offer a definition of feasting in the book's introductory chapter:

> Both of the editors came to the conclusion over a decade ago that feasts are an extremely significant aspect of social life on a worldwide scale, and that understanding them is crucial for apprehending and comprehending many social and cultural processes in ancient societies. ... Feasts are events essentially constituted by the communal consumption of food and/or drink. (2-3)

Further along they write:

> [Feasts] are commonly a central element of life crisis
> ceremonies such as initiations, weddings, and burials.
> (9)

Then, they address the political aspect of feasting as it re-
lates to relations between men and women:

> Feasting frequently involves a gendered asymmetry in
> terms of labor and benefits. That is, very often female
> labor largely supports a system of feasting in which men
> are the primary beneficiaries in the political arena. ...
> These labor inputs are one of the main reasons why there
> is such a strong linkage between polygyny and male
> political power. ... In brief, cases where women provide
> the agricultural, culinary, and serving labor for male
> political activities are quite common. ... However, cases
> of the inverse pattern (where men consistently provide
> the agricultural, culinary, and serving labor that under-
> writes feasts formally hosted by women) may exist, but
> they are extremely rare. (11)

Hayden reminds us that the phenomenon of feasting
assumes the existence of surplus food. It's therefore not
surprising that there is no evidence for this kind of hosted
event among foraging and hunting groups:

> With the emergence of transegalitarian societies (those
> between chiefdoms and true egalitarian societies [i.e.,
> matrilineal clans]), the full range of feasting ... becomes
> established. A range of other developments characterizes
> transegalitarian societies. These developments include
> the production of reliable surpluses, storage of food and
> valuables, private ownership of resources and products,
> the transformation of surpluses into prestige items,
> economically based competition, and the establishment
> of contractual debts. (44)

The occasions for feasting dealt with in *Feasts* range widely from the marking of life-transforming events, such as marriages, to the organization of large work parties (corvée labor), to the attempts at personal prestige-building by individual men. For our purposes, we'll need to concentrate our attention on the economic and political motives that seem common to most of these various occasions.

The politics of the feast

Hayden generalizes that:

> *[T]he drive to achieve advantages through feasting* is probably the single most important impetus behind the intensified production of surpluses beyond household needs for survival. (Hayden's italics; 27)

This assertion may be somewhat of an overstatement, since the utility of access to surplus food in the amelioration of occasional calamities like crop failures would also have provided an impetus for increasing food production. But what, exactly, were the advantages offered by feasting that Hayden refers to?

We mentioned in Chapter 20 the practice of interclan gift exchange, a collective custom among hunters and gatherers whose obligatory nature had the effect of stabilizing interclan relations. The innovation of feasting with the transition to agricultural production can be seen as an elaboration of this earlier practice, but with several important differences.

First, the collective nature of the previous practice is missing. Now, there is an individual male host, backed up, of course, by his family members, who provide the necessary labor for the feast. Second, the usual offerings are no longer token food items given and received, but a more or less elaborate banquet type of event to be enjoyed — and appreciated — by the lucky invited guests. Third, the obvious imbalance of obligation inherent in a feast is somewhat smoothed over by the festive character of the event. But, as they say, the devil will have his due.

Among the various advantages accruing to the hosts that are mentioned by *Feasts'* contributors are 1) social prestige — useful for those seeking increased political authority; 2) wealth — when the guests are made to feel obligated to bring contributions to the feast, the host gets to keep the "leftovers," which may include storable food or luxury items; 3) labor mobilization — the host may make clear that the gratitude felt by the guests must be channeled into a collective work project of benefit to him; and 4) formalizing social inequalities — the men eat first, the women later; the guests eat, the workers serve; the "special guests" get special food, the others get more ordinary food; seating is arranged based on the value of the gift brought by each guest, etc.

Dietler observes:

> The relationship of giver to receiver, or host to guest, translates into a relationship of social superiority and inferiority unless and until the equivalent can be returned. ... In this feature, the potential of hospitality to be manipulated as a tool in defining social relations, lies the crux of commensal [feasting] politics. (74-75)

The feast as an instrument for the exploitation of labor

Regarding so-called "work feasts" in particular, contributors Dietler and Ingrid Herbich note:

> Regardless of the formal ideology of a society, large work feasts that are viewed as a finite exchange transaction with no reciprocal labor obligations can result, in the course of practice, in asymmetrical labor flows, such that some indi-

viduals or households derive wealth and prestige from the labor of others. This fact has profound significance for the long-term development of social relations and economic structures. (257-258)

The practice of holding feasts, along with the other economically based social innovations that we've previously noted [e.g., monogamous marriage], has brought us into a new world, a world dominated by men. The prevalence of feasting in transitional societies appears to have been an important vehicle in establishing the male social, political and economic dominance that relegated wives to the status of field and household slaves.

That said, we need, from this point on, to be mindful that we have entered the time period when human society becomes divided into haves and have-nots, when the contradictory interests of the conflicting social classes are the motive force propelling social change. In a flash of working-class consciousness, Dietler notes that:

> Whatever kings, chiefs, or elite classes are doing with their food, common households will continue to hold feasts in their own way to establish community and personal relationships, mobilize labor, and build symbolic capital. (93)

CHAPTER 22

The 'privatization' of marriage

Where did the innovation of private property — a concept totally alien to gathering and hunting peoples — come from? First, it should be noted that Marxists make a distinction between private property and personal property. Both your toothbrush and your home — if you're lucky enough to have a house with the mortgage paid off — fall within the realm of personal property.

For the foraging woman or the male hunter, her or his tools, weapons, personal ornamentation, ritual gear and other such materials constituted personal property. The customs of pre-class societies concerning disposal of this personal property upon the possessor's death varied. It might be destroyed or buried with her or him or them, or divided among surviving clan members.

One of the "Supplementary Texts" penned by Karl Marx in his book, ***Pre-Capitalist Economic Formations***, includes the passage:

> As the last phase of the primitive formation of society, the agricultural community is at the same time a transitional phase to the secondary formation — i.e., transition from society based on common property to society based on private property. The secondary formation comprises ... the series of societies based on slavery and serfdom. (145)

In *The German Ideology*, a book which Marx and Frederick Engels co-wrote, they further develop this idea:

> The first form of ownership is tribal … ownership. It corresponds to the underdeveloped stage of production, at which a people lives by hunting and fishing, by the rearing of beasts or, in the highest stage, by agriculture. In the latter case it presupposes a great mass of uncultivated stretches of land.
>
> The division of labour is at this stage still very elementary and is confined to a further extension of the natural division of labour existing in the family. The social structure is, therefore, limited to an extension of the family; patriarchal family chieftains, below them the members of the tribe, finally slaves. The slavery latent in the family only develops gradually with the increase of population, the growth of wants, and with the extension of external relations, both of war and of barter. (43-44)

The 'commodification' of human beings

With regard to the institution of slavery, Engels writes the following in *Origin*:

> We saw [in an earlier section of the book] how at a fairly early stage in the development of production, human labor power obtains the capacity of producing a considerably greater product than is required for the maintenance of the producers, and how this stage of development was in the main the same as that in which division of labor and exchange between individuals arises.
>
> It was not long then before the great "truth" was discovered that man can also be a commodity, that human energy can be exchanged and put to use by making a man into a slave. Hardly had men begun to exchange than already they themselves were being exchanged. The active became the passive, whether men liked it or not. (234)

In a related passage, Engels refers to the capture and purchase of women for marriage. Although in this passage he connects the origin and prevalence of these practices to the time when pairing marriage was still the dominant form, the objectification of women that such practices suggest is certainly more characteristic of the onset of patriarchal monogamy. (112)

The factor that may have been in play during this earlier period was the tendency of matrilineal clans to regard both the male and the female members of other clans with whom there were no peaceful contacts as somehow less than human. Evelyn Reed deals with this aspect of early hominin life in her book, *Woman's Evolution.*

In any case, in *Origin*, Engels further contextualizes his view of the evolution of purchase marriage:

> With the preponderance of private over communal property and the interest in its bequeathal, father right and monogamy gained supremacy, the dependence of marriages on economic considerations became complete. The "form" of marriage by purchase disappears; the actual practice is steadily extended until not only the woman but also the man acquires a price — not according to his personal qualities but according to his property. That the mutual affection of the people concerned should be the one paramount reason for marriage, outweighing everything else, was and always had been absolutely unheard of in the practice of the ruling classes; that sort of thing only happened in romance — or among the oppressed classes, who did not count. (142)

Marriage as an instrument bolstering class rule

It will be impossible in this book to deal with the multitude of distinct features that characterized ruling-class marriages in the early kingdoms and empires. However, Stephanie Coontz offers a succinct appraisal of their economic and political basis in her book, *Marriage, a History*:

> More than four thousand years ago a few regional chiefdoms and small-scale warrior societies grew into mighty states in and around the Tigris-Euphrates Valley of the Middle East and the Nile Valley of Africa. Over the next two thousand years other states and empires arose along the Indus and Yellow rivers in India and China respectively, and by 800 B.C., military aristocracies in the Mediterranean region had established several powerful kingdoms there as well. A thousand years later the Mayan empire spread out across Central America. The Aztecs of Mexico and the Incas of South America were relatively latecomers, but they developed in ways similar to their predecessors.
>
> These societies were separated from one another by thousands of years and a myriad of distinctive cultural practices. But in all of them, kings, pharaohs, emperors, and nobles relied on personal and family ties to recruit and reward followers, make alliances, and establish their legitimacy. Marriage was one of the key mechanisms through which such ties were forged. (53)

Thus, as Engels noted in *Origin*, the marriages of the people "who counted," the private property-based rulers under slavery and feudalism, had little or nothing to do with that precious human emotion called love.

Leaving the specific issue of marriage aside for the moment, in the next chapter we take a look at two societies, among many such examples, where the independent processes of social evolution were interrupted and derailed by private property-oriented invaders.

CHAPTER 23

Imperialist intervention brings with it oppression and genocide

In Chapter 16, we noted professor Chris Scarre's estimate that agriculture arose and developed independently in at least seven separate areas of the planet. However, other areas of the planet were not so "lucky." In this chapter, we examine two pre-class societies (out of many hundreds) where the dynamics of autonomous social development were harshly disrupted by outside forces.

Christine Ward Gailey's book, **Kinship to Kingship**, is an impressively detailed analysis of the social evolution of the people of the Tongan Islands, an archipelago in the South Pacific Ocean. The Tongan people were not hunters and gatherers prior to the invasion of European colonialists, but neither had their productive forces as yet brought forth elemental class divisions:

> In precontact Tonga, high rank entitled chiefly people to particular privileges, a greater call on labor and products, rather than ownership of resources or consistent control over nonchiefly people's labor. The critical absence of chiefly control over labor or the determinations of production signaled the non-class nature of the hierarchy. Tongan society was stratified, but the relations of production were kinship-dominated prior to the arrival of Europeans. (54)

Gailey notes:

> The extent and depth of transformation is profound in societies where class relations were only a potentiality, as in Tonga in the later eighteenth century. State formation in Tonga involved a double transformation: a shift from kinship to class relations, and a partial shift from communal and tributary modes of production to a capitalist one. …
>
> In Tonga, the process was catalyzed by merchants' capital and the introduction of Christian ideology. (37)

What forces resisted the development of class inequality prior to the arrival of the colonizers?

> The pivotal position of women, inherent in the principles of kinship ranking, effectively prevented the transformation of Tongan society from kin-based to class-based prior to European intervention. (49)

Women in precontact Tonga enjoyed the kind of rights and privileges we have documented for other pre-class societies.

> Kin, above all the father's sister, greatly influenced the selection of marriage partners. (126)

In the same section, the author cites another investigator who noted that unmarried women "may do as they please, without any shame or disgrace until marriage." (126)

> Sexual activity was not considered either shameful or private, where the parties were unmarried. Brothers and sisters avoided sexual joking in one another's presence, but sexual joking was commonplace for both women and men, in mixed company. (127)

> Child support … was not an issue. Marriage was not an economic necessity for women, whether or not they had children. … They could appropriate their brothers' foodstuffs and valuables to support themselves in a separate household if desired. … Divorced and widowed women were not reproached for having sexual liaisons as they wished. (134)

Most sources agree that Tongan women enjoyed high status relative to European women of the time, and were relatively immune from everyday violence. … Periodic or chronic wife-abuse was exceedingly rare and, at least in some cases, resulted in capital punishment. (137)

Christianity as a reflection and enforcer of patriarchal rule

In the chapter titled "Early Contact," Gailey writes:

Class relations, which are requisite to state formation and dependent upon it for continuity, were catalyzed through … the introduction and extension of Christian ideology, redefinitions of the purpose and consequences of warfare, redefinitions of use-rights and labor claims, the imposition of an uncustomary division of labor, and the creation of a sphere of commodity production. Wesleyan Methodist missionaries provided an ideology of immutable hierarchy (both religious and secular), an impetus for continuous commodity production, and a consistent supply of European weaponry. (145)

Christian proselytizing included forced conversion and the transformation of certain Tongan products into commodities. Both imposed conversion and commoditization eroded women's — particularly nonchiefly women's — sources of autonomy and authority. (170)

The imposition of Western standards of appropriate conduct and arenas of work on Tongan women, coupled with Christian emphasis on husbands' authority and wifely duty, met with intense resistance. The degree of resistance can be gauged by the severity of punishment for infractions. The missionaries attempted to alter traditional sources of women's authority through social pressure, religious instruction, and legal compulsion. (186)

Women went to prison for "fornicating." The missionaries demanded that women cover their breasts. "Illegitimate" children and their mothers were condemned. *Fahu*, the tradition by which women might, for any reason, appropriate for themselves possessions of their brothers and their brothers' children, was condemned and forbidden under missionary-inspired legal codes.

Most importantly, Gailey emphasizes, it was the forceful undermining of women's authority, based on kinship relations, that allowed for the imposition of private property relations:

> What had been a chiefly order was transformed into an aristocracy and a landlord class. ... In short, the land tenure structure fit the description provided by Marx of use rights in an "Asiatic" or tribute-based mode of production. (202)

Short excerpts taken from the chapter on "Changing Production" provide some details:

> Together, forced labor and tax-rent collection constituted the first consistent surplus extraction in the islands. ... After consolidation of political control, the imposition of other commodities, such as textiles, and material support for missionary activities, presented another, more subtle means of undermining production for use. ... The changes in the division of labor by gender, coupled with the import substitution, skewed authority relations in the household and helped create dependency of women upon men. ... The mission station as trading post indicates the deep involvement of the missionaries in the encouragement of commodity production. ... Religious, civil, and commercial institutions created alternative sources of labor in the nineteenth century, including penal servitude, debt bondage, and labor service in tenancy. ... Within the limited wage labor sector in Tonga, the missionary inspired gender division of labor favors male employment, pay scales are much lower for women than for men. (218-239)

This selective summary of Gailey's **Kinship to Kingship** doesn't do full justice to her comprehensive and nuanced analysis of the devolution of Tongan society. Hopefully, though, it sheds some light on the exploitative and oppressive road which numerous communally oriented Indigenous societies have been forced down by the Western imperialist colonizers.

The road to genocide

The savage dismantling of pre-class sociality and communality is a horrific legacy laid down by the market forces of the West. Still more shocking, though, are the many examples globally of full-scale genocide of Indigenous peoples.

We choose here to offer a passage from Canadian author Farley Mowat's *People of the Deer* to portray the appalling, which is to say genocidal, effect of capitalist market forces on Indigenous people around the globe.

Mowat's story of his time in the Arctic lands of the Ihalmiut people west of Canada's Hudson Bay breaks the reader's heart over and over again. Well into his personal narrative, he lets his Ihalmiut friend Ohoto describe the plight of his people:

> In the time of my father we of the People exchanged our spears and our bows for the rifles of white men and in the early years of my youth the rifles gave us meat when we had need, and though the old ways had changed a little, life in this land was still a pleasant thing.
>
> But now, often enough we do not have any shells for the rifles we own, and that seems strange to me. When the white men first came to the edge of our land and told us of the virtues of guns, we believed them. When they told us to put by the ancient deer hunts of our People and turn to the killing of foxes instead, we did what they wished and for a time all was well, and we prospered. Like most of the People I became a fine hunter of foxes from the days of my youth, and I knew all the ways they might be caught. But I did not know much of the hunting of Tuktu

[the great herds of migrating caribou that, for long into the distant past, had been a reliable source of sustenance for the Ihalmiut people] as it was done in the days of my father, for I never needed to know while there were shells for my rifle.

Now, often enough, there are no shells for the rifles, and I cannot tell why, for I still trap many foxes as the white men wished me to do, yet when I take my catch to the wooden igloo in the South, there is no one to greet me but Hikik the squirrel. It was that way first on a winter many years before you came into the land, and I remember the winter well, for the traders told us they must have many foxes that year. They were so anxious that we gave up the great fall hunt of the deer and used all of our skill and our strength to trap foxes, believing we could trade them for food at the place of the white man and so we would have little need of deer meat. But when, in midwinter, we took our pelts south, the door of the wooden igloo stood open and the white man had gone, leaving only the smell which lingered for many long years. Only dead things lay in his camp. The boxes were empty and there was no food in the place and no shells for our guns, so we could not even hunt meat for ourselves.

Indeed I remember that winter, though I wish it would go from my memory. Epeetna, who was my first wife, died during that time and my two children died with her. Nor was I alone in hunger and sorrow for in the camps of the People only one out of five lived to see spring.

Some of those who survived tried to return to the old way of living given to us by Tuktu the deer, but it was found that we did not have the old skills we needed. Some hoped and believed the white man would return and so, stubbornly, clung to their fox traps. These are gone. Only those remained who tried to return to the deer, and few of these are still alive. (136-137)

CHAPTER 24

Women were the first slaves

Chapter 17 dealt generally with the historic innovation of private property, specifically with the treatment of women as property and the use of monogamous marriage as a political and economic tool in the interests of maintaining ruling-class political and economic power in societies based on slave and serf labor.

This chapter will focus on a frequently ignored aspect of the institution of slavery: its origins and economic basis in the exploitation of women. In Gerda Lerner's fact-filled book, *The Creation of Patriarchy*, she devotes a whole chapter to "The Woman Slave." Her general assessment of slavery coincides with that of Karl Marx and Frederick Engels. She writes:

> However oppressive and brutal it undoubtedly was for
> those victimized by it, it represented an essential advance
> in the process of economic organization, an advance upon
> which the development of ancient civilization rested. (76)

The sources of slave labor that she lists are "capture in warfare; punishment for a crime; sale by family members; self-sale for debt; and debt bondage." (76)

With regard to the handling of war captives, Lerner notes the historical evidence contrasting the treatment of men and women. Male captives were most often put to death:

> Even where the economic need for a large slave labor force
> existed there was not enough male labor power available

among the captors to watch over the captives day and night and thus ensure their harmlessness. It would take different peoples different lengths of time to realize that human beings might be enslaved and controlled by other means than brute force. (79)

Captured women suffered a cruel fate

The subjugation of captured women through rape and the severing of their family ties was another matter:

> Since their male kin had been slaughtered, these [women] captives could have no hope of rescue or escape. Their isolation and hopelessness increased their captors' sense of power. The process of dishonoring could in the case of women be combined with the final act of male dominance, the rape of captive women. If a woman had been captured with her children, she would submit to whatever condition her captors imposed in order to secure the survival of her children. If she had no children, her rape or sexual use would soon tend to make her pregnant, and experience would show the captors that women would endure enslavement and adapt to it in the hope of saving their children and eventually improving their lot. (78)

While Lerner has elaborated here a credible basis for the historical precedence of female enslavement before that of men, what is missing is any acknowledgment that, just as some individual women and groups of women must have resisted as best they could the imposition of patriarchal marriage relations, there must have been many examples, unfortunately lost to history (a record, we need to remember, written chiefly by men), of women, individually and in groups, rebelling against their enslavement. (See, for example, the heartwrenching act of infanticide by Sethe in Toni

Morrison's novel *Beloved*. Morrison's story is based on the true-life rebellious act of Margaret Garner, an African-American slave of the antebellum South.)

As Lerner notes, the institutionalization of female slavery had meaning above and beyond its value as a source of unpaid labor power. It also impinged as a social/sexual factor on the gender asymmetry of monogamous marriage:

> Historians writing on slavery all describe the sexual use of enslaved women. … The Babylonian slave woman could also be hired out as a prostitute for a fixed price, sometimes to a brothel owner, sometimes to private clients, with the master collecting her pay. This practice was pervasive throughout the Near East, in Egypt, Greece, and Rome of antiquity, in fact wherever slavery existed. (87)

Further along, she adds:

> There are, of course, in more highly developed slave systems many instances of male slaves being sexually used and abused by master or mistress, but these are exceptions. For women, sexual exploitation marked the very definition of enslavement, as it did not for men. (88-89)

Women's oppression institutionalized in early state societies

With slave women viewed as commodities, it required no great transformation in social values for wives and women in general and their children to be viewed similarly. In the chapters following her exploration of female slavery in early class society, Lerner analyzes at length the Mesopotamian and Hebraic laws accompanying the rise of state-based class societies in southwest Asia and, in particular, the meaning of these laws for women in the context of patriarchal marriage. She summarizes:

We see then, in the thousand-year span we are discussing, how patriarchal dominance moved from private practice into public law. The control of female sexuality, previously left to individual husbands or to family heads, had now become a matter of state regulation. In this, it follows, of course, a general trend toward increasing state power and the establishment of public law. (121)

The laws, of course, were drafted by the slave owners and landlords, potentates of the Middle Eastern city-states and warring empires. The laws legitimized the political power of the rich and shackled their subjects, women and men, slaves and nonslaves alike:

> In the lower-class family, where property was insufficient or nonexistent, persons (children of both sexes) became property and were sold into slavery or degraded marriages. ... All women are increasingly under sexual domination and regulation, but the degree of their unfreedom varies by class. ... The married wife is at one end of the spectrum, the slave woman at the other, the concubine in an intermediate position. (112)

Elaborating on concubinage, Lerner writes:

> Obviously, the increasing importance of keeping private property within the family spurred the development of concubinage as an institution for the preservation of patriarchal property relations. A couple's childlessness, with its implications of loss of property in the male line, could be remedied by bringing a concubine into the household. ... What is of particular interest here is that the concubine serves a dual function: she performs sexual services for the master, with the knowledge and consent of the wife, and she is a servant to the wife. This differs greatly from the relations between first and succeeding wives in many polygamous societies, in which the status of second and third wives is co-equal with that of the first wife. (91-92)

What about marriage among slaves? Orlando Patterson describes its tenuous character in his book, *Slavery and Social Death: A Comparative Study*:

> The refusal formally to recognize the social relations of the slave had profound emotional and social implications. In all slaveholding societies slave couples could be and were forcibly separated and the consensual "wives" of [male] slaves were obliged to submit sexually to their masters; slaves had no custodial claims or powers over their children. (6)

We might note here, as one of the most outrageous and repugnant of the "marriage" practices of slave and feudal society patriarchs, the imposition of "the right of first night." This "custom," whereby the slave owner or feudal landlord could demand and receive sexual access to a subject bride on her wedding night, was dramatically portrayed in Soviet director Sergei Eisenstein's epic, though never completed, film *¡Que Viva México!* Outraged by the affront to their comrade's wife, Mexican peasants living under the feudal dictatorship of Porfirio Díaz organized an armed uprising against the hacienda's owner.

An important reassessment of the role of slavery in social evolution

In her erudite "Introduction" to the 1972 edition of *Origin*, Eleanor Leacock points out that the assertion that there was a stage of human evolution where slave labor became the dominant mode of production replacing communal society is definitely an overstatement. She writes:

> Slavery grew slowly and unevenly in the history of mankind and its significance did not lie in its literal dominance over "free" labor. Greece and Rome were not typical, and although slavery was the first form in which labor was exploited,

primitive communal relations were often transformed into feudal relations without slavery becoming predominant. Engels implies this to be the case in Germany; it seems evident for China and the New World; the French Marxist Maurice Godelier has pointed it out for West African society; and many Soviet scholars seem to be in agreement. (55)

But, as will be noted further along in this book, the kidnapping and enslavement of African people was pivotal for the so-called primitive accumulation of capital that prepared the ground for imperialist domination of the planet.

Photo by Richard Harrington

An Inuit elder rubs noses with a child.

CHAPTER 25

Did communal society survive Europe's Agricultural Revolution?

Was there a golden age of woman-centered peace and plenty during the Neolithic period in the far western region of Eurasia, an area that archaeological theorist Marija Gimbutas labeled "Old Europe"? Gimbutas' hypothesis, presented in a number of books and enthusiastically embraced by numerous feminist writers, envisions a widespread gynocentric society flourishing under the blessings of economic equality and social harmony but, problematically from a materialist point of view, set technologically in the context of the unfolding Agricultural Revolution.

Gimbutas attributes the demise of this Old Europe to an invasion of warriors from the Eastern Steppes, who brought with them the trappings of patriarchy and their Indo-European language and culture. She bases her hypothesis on the results of her own extensive European archaeological fieldwork, the findings of other archaeologists in the Eastern Mediterranean and Middle Eastern areas, an analysis of religious beliefs and myths in those areas, and generally known facts about the prehistory of the areas.

Gimbutas is widely known among feminist scholars for her interpretation of what she terms "goddess figurines." This diverse array of human shapes in stone, bone and clay, many of them with clearly feminine features, are frequent finds at archaeological digs, and Gimbutas marshals them all as evidence for her hypothesized prehistoric gynocentric society in *The Language of the Goddess*. Her description of marriage in Old Europe pretty much parallels what has been written in this book about the pairing marriage form found in matrilineal clan societies previous to the adoption of agriculture.

Challenges to the "Old Europe" hypothesis

Gimbutas' hypothesis has proved to be very controversial. Many archaeologists have challenged her conclusions, and not all these responses have had a reactionary, antifeminist subtext.

In 1993, archaeologist Ian Hodder took up the excavation of a prehistoric Anatolian site called Çatalhöyük, the remains of a 9,000-year-old "town." This work was begun in 1961 by James Mellaart (1925-2012), whose preliminary discoveries there form an important part of Gimbutas' evidence. Hodder, in a book-length report of his own work at that site titled *The Leopard's Tale*, respectfully disagrees with Mellaart's earlier conclusions and Gimbutas' use of them. Another challenge to Gimbutas has come in the form of essays by 12 women archaeologists collected under the title *Ancient Goddesses: The Myths and the Evidence*. (Goodison and Morris 1999)

It remained for a revolutionary Marxist, however, to present a thoroughgoing critique of Gimbutas' hypothesis. As a militant woman leader and a Marxist theorist, Dorothy Ballan was very interested in what Gimbutas had to say. In her article on Gimbutas' hypothesis, "When Goddesses Ruled:

'The Language of the Goddess' Confirms Early Matriarchy" (In *Liberation and Marxism*, June/July 1990), Ballan credits Gimbutas' remarkable achievement:

> The very fact that a woman has broken through the almost inaccessible male-dominated field of archaeology is in itself a considerable accomplishment and a source of pride and encouragement to other women. (2)

Ballan acknowledges Gimbutas' conception of what Ballan terms "an idealized version of ancient primitive communism" as a positive contribution, but notes:

> It is not a new [idea]. This idea was expounded more than a century ago by Bachofen in *Mother Right* and by Lewis Morgan in *Ancient Society*. These forerunners of Gimbutas, who analyzed early society with the information available at that time, were basically correct. But surprisingly, they are not mentioned in Gimbutas' book. (2)
>
> Bachofen, Morgan and Engels laid the foundation for *The Language of the Goddess*. What then is Marija Gimbutas' contribution? What she did was unearth physical evidence that they were right, that the matriarchy did precede the patriarchy. (3)

Eurocentrism and anti-communism tarnish her findings

However, her idealized focus on the matrilineal societies of Stone Age Europe leads to a distorted view of human history. Today a Eurocentric view of world history is justifiably under attack by progressive historians and social scientists. Gimbutas' descriptions of "our authentic European heritage" destroyed by "that aggressive male invasion" from Russia and Asia introduces a narrow Eurocentric view of prehistory.

Gimbutas is an archaeologist with 30-years experience who speaks 17 languages. She cannot be unaware of the research of numerous other anthropologists, archaeologists and historians who have confirmed the worldwide evidence of matrilineal and matriarchal societies. …

Gimbutas presents the overthrow of the matriarchy as though it were merely a case of external force intervening in a peaceful, stable and egalitarian system. She has no other explanation for the great, historic and decisive development that brought about the patriarchy. She dare not give any explanation that deals with the material conditions of life, i.e., with the basic economic conditions in human society. …

The material conditions of life, the growth of the productive forces of society and the relations of production that grow out of it, have no relevance to her cultural theory. The view that technology … in turn changes all the old relations in society, including art and literature, seems not to influence Gimbutas' thinking at all. (3-4)

Female figure from Japan, Jōmon period, 1000-800 B.C.E.

Material forces are the basis for beliefs, social change

Ballan continues:

> It is important to study the forms of ownership in any society to get to the root cause of development, which includes not only upward, forward movement, but also includes regression. What did destroy the primitive form of communism and matrilineal relations in the period of mother right was the beginning of surplus and the private ownership of that surplus.
>
> The beginning of existence of these new conditions corresponds roughly to the rise of the patriarchy. The very social relations that had existed for so long became a brake upon the society and that stagnation led to erosion of the old family relations. It was a development on a world scale, not an external force invading an idyllic society. It was an outgrowth of the stagnation of the older forms of social relations. (4)

Ballan notes and condemns the anti-communist tirade that concludes *The Language of the Goddess*:

> Gimbutas turns to crude anti-communism as a prop for her thesis. This may be music to the ears of the ultraright in the United States and it may help in gaining favorable press reviews. But it will do little to establish her work as a significant contribution — either to archaeology or to the women's movement.
>
> Another problem is what many reviewers praise as the spiritual implications of her work. … It is all good and well for women to be inspired by the facts, established more than a century ago, that matriarchal, communal societies flourished widely for many, many thousands of years. … But Gimbutas climbs to another dimension altogether when she glorifies divine female worship as the force behind egalitarian, communal societies. She implies that myths determine the basis of society, rather than the social and economic basis of society determining the myths. This

> puts her work in the field of myth and superstition. It also puts her in conflict with science. (5)

Taking into consideration Ballan's incisive evaluation and the well-reasoned misgivings of many of Gimbutas' archeological colleagues, we think it's safe to conclude that Gimbutas' hypothesis (as opposed to the findings of her fieldwork) does not represent a defensible exception to a materialist perspective on the evolution of patriarchal society.

As human groups in Europe and elsewhere adopted agricultural production over foraging and hunting as their primary source of sustenance, the new relations of production introduced economic inequality that favored men over women. What Gimbutas' work actually uncovered are significant cultural and material vestiges of the communal human society that was no longer dominant in her hypothesized "Old Europe" of the Neolithic period.

In future chapters our attention will be drawn to the tenacious persistence of some other pre-patriarchal "vestiges" well into the epoch of patriarchy and the efforts of patriarchal rulers to stamp them out.

CHAPTER 26

Marriage comes under the control of the state

The widespread employment of agricultural production in certain areas of the planet generated great wealth in those areas. The minority who took possession of this wealth developed a variety of strategies to maintain their booty and their privileged status.

The creation of patriarchal religions represented one such strategy. The authority of priestly figures standing on high platforms above the masses to summon supernatural powers superseded the authority of village headmen and found common cause with warrior leaders. The tenets of patriarchal religion brought a message to the masses that male supremacy and economic and social inequality were simply the natural order of things.

The rise of powerful city-states in Mesopotamia, the region in southwest Asia between the Tigris and Euphrates rivers, was illustrative of another strategy, this one based on the development of a warrior caste and the employment of the material threat of physical force. The city-states of Sumer are most often cited as the first appearance of "civilization."

The Marxist view of 'the state'

The existence of a repressive force beholden to the wealthy in all class societies was analyzed in detail by the great communist leader, V. I. Lenin. His written work on this subject, *The State and Revolution*, has stood for a hundred years as the definitive guide to understanding the role of the state as the pre-eminent instrument of class domination and control.

Drawing on the original formulations of Karl Marx and Frederick Engels decades earlier, Lenin paraphrases:

> The state is the product and the manifestation of the *irreconcilability* of class antagonisms. The state arises when, where and to the extent that class antagonisms objectively *cannot* be reconciled. And conversely, the existence of the state proves that the class antagonisms are irreconcilable. … According to Marx, the state is an organ of class *rule*, an organ for the *oppression* of one class by another; it is the creation of "order," which legalizes and perpetuates this oppression by moderating the conflict between the classes. … A standing army and police are the chief instruments of state power. (Lenin's italics; 8-10)

So it was with the city-states of Mesopotamia and, later, in a few other relatively densely populated areas of the planet where states arose. J. M. Roberts in **The New Penguin History of the World** notes:

> Somewhere in the fourth millennium B.C. is the starting-point of the story of civilizations. … We begin with the first recognizable civilization in Mesopotamia. The next example is in Egypt, where civilization is observable at a slightly later date, perhaps about 3100 B.C. Another marker in the Near East is "Minoan" civilization, which appears in Crete in about 2000 B.C. … Meanwhile, further east and perhaps around 2500 B.C., another civilization has appeared in India. … China's first civilization starts later, towards the middle of the second millennium B.C. Later still come the meso-Americans. (42)

All these centers of wealth accumulation witnessed the rise of what Engels called "a special public power," or, in Lenin's words, "special bodies of armed men which have prisons, etc., at their command."

Legal infringements on the freedom of women

In Mesopotamia, as elsewhere, the evolution of state power was accompanied by legal restrictions on the institution of marriage, as first seen in the Code of Hammurabi. While having mostly to do with property considerations — patriarchy demanded that the inheritance of property through the male line be guaranteed — these laws already reflected the misogynistic brutality that has been so typical of patriarchal rule.

In her book *The Creation of Patriarchy*, Gerda Lerner describes the plight of Mesopotamian women accused of adultery:

> For women even the accusation of adultery could prove fatal. If the husband so accused his wife before a court, she could vindicate herself by taking an oath. … If, however, the accusation came not from her husband but from others in the community, the wife could vindicate herself only by undergoing the ordeal, that is, she had to "leap into the river for her husband," … The river-god would then decide on her guilt or innocence. (115)

And further along she notes:

> The various laws against rape all incorporated the principle that the injured party is the husband or the father of the raped woman. The victim was under an obligation to prove that she had resisted the rape by struggling or shouting. (116)

For ruling-class figures in these early states, marriageable daughters became pawns in efforts at further wealth amassment, interstate diplomacy and alliance building. In Stephanie Coontz's *Marriage, a History*, we read:

> Whereas heads of state today ratify treaties with a signature and ceremonial stamp, rulers — or aspiring rulers — of the past often sealed their deals with a marriage ceremony. …

> Few rulers took account of their children's desires when they arranged such political marriages. (54-55)

Further along she writes that:

> Many families voluntarily offered their daughters or sisters to rulers with the aim of gaining a useful family connection. (56)

She cites examples of these practices in the early state societies of Egypt, China, Mexico, Greece and Rome.

Coontz also comments on the economic manipulation of marriage among the general populations of these states:

> In the kingdoms of the ancient world, marriage was important for the common folk as well. In the millennia before the development of banks and free markets, marriage was the surest way for people lower down the social scale to acquire new sources of wealth, add workers to family enterprises, recruit business partners, and preserve or pass on what they already had. People who aspired to even the lowest rungs of government office often found it crucial to contract a marriage with the "right" set of in-laws. Intensified demands for tribute and taxes forced peasants to choose mates and in-laws who could help them increase agricultural production. (54)

But the dominance of patriarchy was always evident:

> In ancient Athens, if a woman became an heiress (this could happen only if her father died without leaving a son), she could be claimed as a bride by her closest male relative, even if she was already married, in order to keep the property within the family. If the kinsman who claimed the heiress was also married, he could summarily divorce his wife. (65)

This overtly economic and political rationale underlying marriage in early state societies has continued as a fundamental motive for this institution's use up to the present.

CHAPTER 27

Patriarchal heterosexual marriage under slavery and feudalism

In *Marriage, a History,* author Coontz suggests that one of the objectives of patriarchal political domination was to stamp out the vestiges of matrilineal kinship solidarity that still manifested themselves in the form of competing family coalitions and dynasties:

> Ultimately, none of [the patriarchal ruling-class] efforts succeeded in displacing the marriage alliance system from its central role in politics and economics.
>
> But three attempts to curtail aristocratic family power eventually had particular significance for the development of marriage in Western Europe. The first was the establishment of democracy [for slave-owning and property-owning men] in Athens in the fifth century B.C. The second was the imposition of universal law and the development of a professional army in the Roman Republic and early empire. A third came in the later days of the Roman Empire, when Christianity emerged as an institution that combined a universal ideal of brotherhood with many trappings of state power. (70)

The state takes control

As one example of this effort in "democratic" Athens, Coontz notes:

> Inheritance claims based solely on blood descent were no longer sufficient; a state-sanctioned marriage of the parents was now required. (72)

What was the underlying objective of this and other legal stipulations?

> Athenian leaders were anxious to convert marriage into an association of two individuals rather than two kin groups. (75)

Coontz reports a striking reversal from traditional marriage practice during the period of Republican Rome:

> As early as 230 B.C., dowries given to husbands had replaced bridewealth paid to the bride's family as the prevailing financial arrangement in Roman weddings. For the life of the marriage the husband controlled the dowry, but he had to return it in the event of divorce, unless the woman had been blatantly promiscuous. (81-82)

As is so generally characteristic of patriarchal society, evidently no importance was attached to "blatant promiscuity" on the part of the husband.

Coontz also makes the point that Rome's imperial preoccupations required a professional army and a civilian bureaucracy of colonial administrators, effectively curtailing the political power of landowning families and family alliances.

Patriarchal religion as a repressive force

With the evolution of early Christianity from the original set of beliefs held by a rebellious Semitic sect into a powerful state religion in late Imperial Rome, we encounter the full blossoming of the poisonous weed of patriarchal sexual hypocrisy and repression. Coontz cites a couple of the most well-known precepts of the Church Fathers:

> "It is better," [the Apostle] Paul grudgingly conceded, "to marry than to burn" (Corinthians 7:9). Pope Gregory the Great [c. 540-604 C.E.] explained early in the sixth century that although marriage was not sinful, "conjugal union cannot take place without carnal pleasure, and such pleasure cannot under any circumstances be without blame." (86)

How much personal emotional torment over the centuries resulted from these absurd pontifications cannot be measured, but they were very much on the mark as ideological accompaniments to patriarchal political rule. The Catholic Church is or at least should be infamous for its zealous and at times murderous efforts to impose strict sexual abstinence on its flock, excepting only heterosexual, penile-vaginal intercourse between partners married by the church and motivated solely by the need to produce a new generation of faithful parishioners.

Of course, the Vatican, as sordid as its long history is, has not stood alone. All of the influential and still existing religious institutions that arose as reflections of patriarchal rule sought to curtail the social and sexual rights of the masses, but most especially of women.

We're going to skip over Coontz's detailed account of the Church's manipulation of its marriage tenets as an important weapon in its maneuverings with the feudal nobility of medieval Europe. The Church itself, as the continent's chief landowner, was a major player in the interminable power struggles of that epoch.

Coontz also, however, deals at length with what she terms "the other 95 percent":

> For the first eight centuries of its existence, the church itself showed little concern about what made for a valid marriage or divorce among the lower classes of society. Gradually, however, all social classes came to live by the rules for forming and dissolving marriages that had emerged out of the conflicts and compromises among monarchs, nobles, and various factions of the church during the early medieval period. (104)

Coontz notes that among Europe's peasants:

> The Church was dealing with a population whose traditions considered mutual intent or the blessing of a parent sufficient to solemnize a marriage. (106)

But in 1215, the Church's Fourth Lateran Council declared:

> "[W]e absolutely prohibit clandestine marriages." For a marriage to be valid, the council stated, three things were necessary: The bride had to have a dowry, which effectively undercut the independence of a young woman from her parents; banns [the marriage announcement] had to be published beforehand; and the wedding had to take place in a church. (106-107)

And even though a less strict doctrine eventually prevailed:

> When the Gregorian reformers really began to flex their muscles on the question of no marriage for the clergy and no divorce for the laity, Church law no longer made any provision for divorce at all. (108)

Preoccupation with inheritance, other economic concerns

The feudal barons exercised their own secular authority over the social/sexual relations of their serfs:

In some regions the lord of an estate (or the abbot if a peasant worked on church lands) could prevent his serf from marrying a woman from another manor. In other regions, lords even had the right to choose husbands for their tenants' daughters. (110)

Coontz explains the economic motive behind these harsh interventions:

Landowners had a stake in their serfs' marriages because the division of labor between husband and wife lay at the heart of rural economies. No individual, male or female, could run a farm single-handedly. (110)

And at the level of the individual family:

By law, husbands controlled all household resources, including any earnings wives brought in, and could "discipline" their wives by force if necessary. … Marriage in urban areas followed many of the same patterns. (114)

Unfortunately, Coontz's information about the conditions of marriage in peasant-based societies in other parts of the world is rather limited. She writes:

In the areas of classic patriarchy, such as the Middle East, North Africa, India and China, where girls are married at very young ages and placed in households headed by their husbands' fathers, a woman can gain leverage in the family only by producing male heirs. (131)

In India, early law codes provided that a widow with no sons had to marry her husband's brother in order to produce a male child to carry on his lineage. (46)

Regarding attitudes toward marriage in feudal China:

In Confucian philosophy, the two strongest relationships in family life are between father and son and between elder brother and younger brother, not between husband and wife. In thirteenth century China the bond between father and son was so much stronger than the bond between husband and wife that legal commentators insisted a couple do nothing if the patriarch of the household raped his son's wife. (21)

Coontz pulls from a "women's issues" report that appeared in several U.S. newspapers in 2004 the fact that:

[F]or 1,700 years women in one Chinese province guarded a secret language that they used to communicate with each other about the griefs of marriage. (22)

CHAPTER 28

Same-sex love and 'marriage' in pre-capitalist class society

In Chapter 15 we dealt with manifestations of same-sex marriage in pre-class societies. We limited that survey to societies where foraging and hunting still prevailed as the dominant mode for providing sustenance at the time that same-sex pairings were observed by outsiders. Wanting to project backward in time to the distant millennia when hominins were just becoming human, our reasoning was that life patterns in societies still untouched by the Agricultural Revolution provided firmer ground for inferences about that distant past.

A less strict criterion would have opened the door to many more reports — by explorers, missionaries, soldiers, entrepreneurs, colonizers and anthropologists — that include data on nontransient homosexual and transgender/nonbinary pairings among members of transitional societies and early agricultural societies in Africa, Asia, Oceania, Australia and the Americas. Unfortunately, though, once we reach the early class-stratified states, the material on same-sex marriage focuses mostly on the lives of the wealthy and powerful.

Ascendancy of ruling-class attitudes toward sexual behavior

Bruce Trigger (1937-2006) was a renowned Canadian archaeologist, anthropologist and ethnohistorian. He is the author of *Understanding Early Civilizations*, a comparative study of seven early class societies: Mesopotamia, Egypt, Shang China, the Aztecs, the Mayas, the Incas and the Yoruba. In the several pages of his book devoted to a discussion of homosexuality, we find a largely negative assessment of sexual behavior among these peoples: "In general, people in early civilizations considered reproduction the primary goal of sexual activity." (190) Really? His evidence for this assertion is a mishmash of contradictory practices and attitudes, most probably reflecting differing attitudes of the different social classes.

What can be gleaned from his analysis is that the ruling classes of these early states gave the reproduction of their subject populations a high priority, both as sources of labor and tribute, through taxation and otherwise, and as cannon fodder for their military campaigns. The atomized character of patriarchal families suited them just fine:

> People depended on their children to take care of them in their old age, and the domestic division of labour provided a strong incentive for both men and women to marry. (190)

The communal safety and security guaranteed by the communal clan was long gone. Each family was on its own. The patriarchal family had become the basic economic unit of society.

In such a milieu, most social/sexual patterns outside of male-dominated, state-sanctioned marriage were viewed unfavorably — a notable exception being the institution of concubinage that served rich men. But Trigger also makes reference, as have other investigators, to the inclusion in early state religious practices of ritual sexuality (arguably a holdover from hunter-gatherer culture), which included homosexual and transgender couplings. Prominent among leading religious figures associated with the ruling stratum were homosexuals and gender-variant people. He also mentions homosexuals and gender-variant people among the servants and entertainers in royal courts. Did these people's personal lives include life partners? Did they produce and/or raise children?

Same-sex marriage in some pre-capitalist societies

An unusually rich source of historical information about same-sex marriage is James Neill's *The Origins and Role of Same-Sex Relations in Human Societies*. Neill's discussion of same-sex relations in ancient Greece includes the following observations:

> A character in Plato's *Symposium* alludes to the variations in attitudes to homosexual love among the other Greek states when he contrasts the situation in Athens, which he characterizes as "complicated" due to the restraints imposed upon the partners, with the customs in Elis and Boetia, where he says homosexual love was unfettered by the sort of moral considerations present in Athens. Xenophon, in fact, wrote that in Boetia and other Greek states homosexuality was so unrestrained that men and boys "were living together like married couples." (170)

Concerning love among women in early Greece, Neill writes:

> Most of what is known about love between women in ancient Greece comes … from the great poetess, Sappho. … For most of her life she was the head of a "thiasoi," an association of young women, found not only on Lesbos, but

An artist's conception of a meeting of ancient women, perhaps
a depiction of a thiasoi gathering.

in other areas of Greece. … [The thiasoi] were communities
in which adolescent girls learned dance, music and singing.
… They were groups with their own divinities and rituals
where girls went through a transforming experience of life
that was somewhat analogous to that experienced by males
in initiation rituals. … In the seventh and sixth centuries
[B.C.E.] love relations between women were not only an
accepted feature of life in the thiasoi, but they were
formalized in an initiation-type ritual that brought two
girls together in a sexual union similar to a marriage. (161)

And in classical Rome:

Sexual relationships between women, while not as common [as among men], also appear in literature of the
period. … Though sparse, there are enough references to
female homosexuality in the literature produced in the
first several centuries of the Empire to suggest that, like
male homosexuality, it was a common occurrence, and not
an exceptional situation. (207)

Neill summarizes the plots of several literary pieces of the period that deal with lesbian marriages and then comments:

> As the references to the marriages between women mentioned in these stories suggest, formal marriages between same-sex couples were not uncommon among Romans during the Empire. … Rather than the unrestrained sexual promiscuity that many today associate with the Roman Empire, the popular literature of the period reveals the same interest in romantic love and committed relationships among Roman writers and their audiences as among people in our own time. The only difference between the two societies in this regard is that to the Romans such a committed and emotionally fulfilling sexual relationship could be had just as easily with a member of the same sex as the opposite sex. (207-208)

Neill writes that the Ming dynasty in China (A.D. 1368-1644) witnessed a weakening of imperial court influence on the government and its replacement by a professional bureaucracy:

> Instead of the lives of the court aristocracy which had been the principal focus of the literature of earlier periods, stories and novels of the Ming deal with the lives and loves of ordinary Chinese — shopkeepers, soldiers, poets and minor officials — and provide us with a view of a society in which homosexual loves existed side by side with the social obligations of heterosexual marriage. (257)
>
> Ming literature … detailed the ways in which women could find sexual satisfaction with each other. … Marriage relationships between women were not uncommon in some regions. In a typical relationship, two women, one designated the "husband" and the other the "wife," would formalize their union in a ceremony in which they would exchange gifts, as was the practice in normal heterosexual marriage ceremonies. At the conclusion of the ritual the female friends of the couple who witnessed the ceremony

would join them in a feast. The two married women sometimes adopted female children, who were then entitled to inherit property from the parents of the couple.

Evidence from Ming literature, then, shows that homosexuality among women was very likely just as frequent ... as among men during the period. Given the lack of prohibitions against homosexuality from the earliest dynasties, it seems probable that same-sex love would have been as common among women as it had been among men down through the course of Chinese history, even though the orientation of the literature around the lives of men caused it to be rarely mentioned before the time of the Ming. (262)

Our focus in this chapter has been limited to a number of references to the persistence of same-sex marriage in several pre-capitalist societies. That homosexual behavior was widespread in all societies based on slavery and serfdom has been documented by many scholars. That such sexual and gender-variant behavior came under increasing proscription in many of these societies has also been documented. In the next chapter, we'll examine the operation of some of these repressive forces.

CHAPTER 29

Sexual repression as an instrument of class domination

The ruling classes of the early state societies had written legal codes that "legitimized" their power, property and privileges, and that circumscribed and curtailed the rights of their subjects. Behind these legal documents stood what gave the laws their teeth: the threat of punitive physical force, up to and including death, for violations. The mere existence of the rulers' "armed bodies of men" was usually sufficient to guarantee "obedience" by the masses. But history also records examples of popular armed rebellions against the king's bullies.

In Chapter 26 we noted that the tenets of patriarchal religions brought a message to the masses that male supremacy and economic and social inequality were the natural order of things. A separate but similarly motivated message had to do with sexual relations. Religious challenges to the idea that sexual relations were a natural part of life and something to be enjoyed figure most prominently in the history of Christianity as it evolved from a rebellious sect into a powerful instrument of exploitation and repression for use by the European ruling classes.

Sexual repression through religious doctrine

Patriarchal religious doctrine provided a complementary and highly efficient resource for ruling-class control. To the external threat of physical repression, Christianity and other patriarchal religions added an internalized "conscience" of what was "moral" and what was not. In James Neill's *The Origins and Role of Same-Sex Relations in Human Societies*, we find a concise description of the evolution of Catholic Church teachings on sex and marriage:

> A common characteristic of the clerical reformers who began assembling the ecclesiastical opinions, penitentials, patristic writings, and the edicts and decrees of church councils into the first collections of canon law was an undisguised horror of sexual activity. ... The ascetic reformers ... were convinced that to achieve salvation it was necessary to be freed from the evil of sex. They not only took a vow of chastity, but strove to eliminate even sexual thoughts from their minds. (361)

Citing another authority on the issue, Neill emphasizes:

> "[The reformers] were not merely suspicious of sex, but hostile to any sexual activity at all, save for marital relations undertaken expressly and consciously to conceive a child." In their zeal for sexual purity, the reformers went beyond even the asceticism of the early church Fathers, and were determined to limit marital sex to the absolute minimum, and on penalizing extra-marital sex as harshly as possible. (361)

Neill writes that the Catholic Church's campaign to abolish marriage among priests and nuns was hard fought over several centuries:

> Marriage by members of the clergy, theoretically forbidden since the 5th century, was singled out for condemna-

tion in statutes passed by the Council of Mainz presided over by Pope Leo IX in 1054. [Pope Gregory VII's] statute forbade non-celibate priests from officiating at mass, prohibited clergy who were still married from having any sexual intercourse at all, and required that married clergy who did not immediately separate from their wives be defrocked. …

Resistance to the church's efforts to abolish clerical marriage and enforce celibacy among the clergy was fierce and widespread. Defiance of the ban, in fact, would persist for nearly two centuries before it was established with finality across Europe. (370-371)

In *The Roots of Lesbian and Gay Oppression*, the present author noted the pecuniary basis for the ban:

It is of interest in this regard that the Church's demand for celibacy of its priests and nuns had more to do with financial than moral considerations. The Church sought to ensure that it would be the only legitimate heir for whatever wealth its ordained members might possess. (27)

He also described the evolving position of the feudal Church in Europe with regard to homosexuality:

At first, the anti-homosexual position of the Church was manifested mainly in warnings, such as this one addressed to a group of nuns in 423 by St. Augustine: "The love which you bear to one another ought not to be carnal." Soon, however, the clerical prohibitions acquired a more serious character. By 693, the Church in Spain was reaffirming [Emperor] Justinian's punishment for male homosexuality [dating from 538]: castration followed by execution. New penalties for homosexuality among nuns were also being devised although they were not as severe as the penalties for male clerics.

By the 11th century, if not earlier, the Church had begun supplementing its "flexible" approach among the pagans

> with increased repression. … [Arthur] Evans [1978] and other investigators have described the existence of groups that continued to practice old, matriarchal religious rites in many parts of feudal Europe. Often, an "Earth Mother" goddess or other such female deity was the central figure of worship. If there were male deities, they were usually explicitly phallic. There is also evidence of ritual transvestism among some of these groups. These movements tended to reject the prevailing values that called for the subjugation of women and the persecution of homosexuality. In fact, there is a good deal of evidence that the ritual sexuality of their religious rites included homosexual practices. Some of these groups were openly hostile to the Church and state, challenging the need for a clergy, a government, marriage or an organized religious hierarchy. (28-29)

If the Vatican's view of connubial bliss among both the heterosexual and the homosexual laity and clergy of Europe was harsh, its posture with regard to any kind of sexual activity outside of church-sanctioned marriage proved to be tyrannical and genocidal and global in scope.

Taking from James Neill's detailed account just a sampling from the church's centuries-long campaign against "sodomy," we read:

> The fourth Lateran Council, convened by [Pope] Innocent III in 1215, brought one of the largest ever assemblages of church leaders to Rome. (378)

The decrees passed at this church council included the establishment of what would become the Office of the Inquisition, a requirement that Jews wear special identifying dress, a crusade "to restore the Holy Land to Christian rule," and a restatement of the demand for celibacy:

> [T]he end result of the initiatives undertaken by Innocent III was the creation by the late 13th century of a religious

tyranny overseen by the papacy, and enforced not only by the Inquisition, but by the newly organized mendicant orders [church groups whose members were sworn to poverty], who made it their business to seek out and punish sexual nonconformists, intellectual dissidents or anyone else who fell outside of the papacy's vision of a Christian society ruled by God's law as dictated by the pope. (378)

Neill describes in detail numerous examples of the horrors that befell hapless individual victims of the Inquisition, but the campaign also included mass killings, as happened, for example, with the massacre of an estimated 7,000 men, women and children in the French town of Beziers. The town was known as a center of the Cathar heresy. The Cathars were one of a number of mass movements in medieval Europe that challenged the anti-sex doctrines of the Catholic Church. These groups appear to have maintained pre-patriarchal religious beliefs and practices, including ritual sexuality by members of the same sex. Therefore, they were special targets for Vatican repression.

Sexual repression had a class basis

Unfortunately, Neill offers only a psychological basis for the crimes of the Catholic Inquisition. He is undoubtedly correct that sexual repression is an important genesis for psychopathology. But the roots of the European anti-sex campaign were not to be found in the pathology of one or a handful of deranged individuals. The Vatican clear headedly oversaw a continent-wide organization and was Europe's prime landowner in this period. The Vatican at times competed and at other times cooperated with the secular nobility of Europe. Its paramount goal was to continue amassing wealth and preserving its political power. It used both organized violence and the internalization of sexual guilt, by which means it weakened the ability of the masses to unite and resist its harsh rule.

But is our focus on the Catholic Church, with its center in Rome, and Christianity in general an example of a one-sided Eurocentric analysis? We think not. The anti-sexual doctrines of Roman Catholicism at first represented an attack on the social/sexual living patterns practiced by the European masses. Finding them useful in controlling the people, the rulers then had the same sexually repressive doctrines exported all over the world by Catholic and other Christian missionaries as the imperial powers of Europe sought world conquest.

What follows is a small sampling of the crimes perpetrated on an almost global basis by the self-appointed representatives of Jesus Christ, who were, in reality, obvious servitors of the European colonial masters.

Ramón Gutiérrez's book, *When Jesus Came, the Corn Mothers Went Away: Marriage, Sexuality, and Power in New Mexico, 1500-1846*, documents the great harm caused to the Indigenous peoples of then-northern Mexico by the Spanish invaders' religious fanaticism. In the section of his book titled "Franciscan Evangelism," he writes:

> If the [Pueblo] Indians were to reach God, they too would
> have to be led through purgation, illumination, and union.
> This clearly emerges when the friars outlined their mission
> in New Mexico as that of leading the Indians "out from the
> darkness of paganism and the somberness of death" and
> into the "Father of Light."
>
> The purgation of the Indian's soul began with a
> systematic repudiation of Pueblo religion. The Indians
> had to renounce Satan, banish his earthly assistants
> (Native chiefs), and forsake their superstitious beliefs and

idols. To assure that the Indians did not cling to their idolatry the friars raided homes, confiscated katsina dolls, ceremonial masks, prayer sticks, and fetishes. …

Once the visible forms of idolatry had been destroyed, the friars turned their attention to the wretched sins of the flesh. Sex in Pueblo society was a positively valued activity that assured social and cosmic reproduction. Few restrictions were placed on sexual pleasures, and certainly guilt and remorse were not associated with such activities. …

The Puebloans practiced serial monogamy and polygamy, and seemed undisturbed by sexual variance. The main distinctions the Christian lexicon had to describe Indian sexual practices were those of sin. Thus the Pueblo *berdaches*, those half-men—half-women who symbolized cosmic harmony, were simply *putos* (male whores) and *sodomitas* (sodomites) to the Spanish. Even the position in which the Indians copulated was "bestial." …

The laws of God commanded chastity before marriage, fidelity within the nuptial state, life-long indissoluble monogamy, and modesty and shame in all bodily matters. Men and women who practiced "bestial" activities, who wallowed in their pagan promiscuity, violating Christian laws of sexual morality, had to be publicly whipped, placed in stocks, and sheared of their locks. (Gutiérrez's italics; 71-73)

Missionary malevolence in Kenya and Tahiti

In the book-length collection of essays edited by Peter Drucker titled **Different Rainbows**, we find Kenya-born John Mburu's contribution under the title "Awakenings: Dreams and Delusions of an Incipient Lesbian and Gay Movement in Kenya" (179-191). On the subject of sexual freedom, he writes:

It is evident that the notion of exclusive heterosexuality in pre-colonial sub-Saharan Africa is not borne out by the evidence. Though same-sex practices were not met with social approval in all African societies, it is clear that in many communities same-sex relations were closely interwoven in the social fabric. In some cases, as with the institution of *jin bandaa*, transvestite homosexuals played a significant role in the community. ...

With one of the fastest growing church populations in the world, Africa is pervaded by the influence of Christian doctrine opposed to homosexuality. Early evangelizing missions surreptitiously meshed traditional African customary belief systems with biblical scripture. ... African practices that were considered an abomination — such as levirate, a practice in which widows would marry their deceased husband's brother; female circumcision; woman-woman marriage; and homosexuality — were stamped out or driven underground. ...

Kenya's archaic penal code dates back to the era of British colonial rule. While in Britain penalties against "crimes against nature" were repealed in 1967, these vestiges of Kenya's colonial past still remain intact. (Mburu's italics; 182-184)

Another example of missionary interference in the social/sexual lives of Indigenous peoples comes from Niko Besnier's contribution to the book *Third Sex, Third Gender: Beyond Sexual Dimorphism in Culture and History* (Herdt 1996: 285-328). Besnier writes:

For Europeans of the Enlightenment and early Romantic era, Polynesia, one of the last frontiers of colonial expansionism, was the embodiment of a paradise. (288)

But soon enough, European perceptions of Polynesia changed course. Particularly as the London Missionary Society was being established in Tahiti, vanguarding massive missionary endeavors throughout Polynesia for years to come, the island turned, in the eyes of foreigners, from the New Cythera [a name given Tahiti by a French explorer] to "the filthy Sodom of the South Seas." ... Besides infanticide, human sacrifice and adultery … one feature of Tahitian society particularly captured the missionaries' attention. … The Tahitians' "predilection" for "sodomy" had already been amply described in seafarers' journals. … George Hamilton, surgeon on the British frigate Pandora, who spent three weeks on the island, had remarked in 1791 that young men were kept "for abominable purposes." (290-291)

British seamen and missionaries of the Georgian era [the 18th and early 19th century period of British global expansion] evaluated the practices of which they caught glimpses in Tahiti through a specific framework of moral reference. In the late eighteenth century, "sodomy" had become the focus of particularly virulent revilement in England. As is well documented, sodomy was an "utterly confused category" into which fell many "unnatural practices," principally homosexual and heterosexual oral or anal intercourse and bestiality. (293)

Much more documentation for the dissemination of anti-sexual propaganda and repression throughout Indigenous North America, South America, Africa, Oceania and Asia on the part of professional proselytizers for patriarchal religions is available. In the next chapter, we focus a Marxist lens on the issue of gender.

Photo Dianna Davies

Marsha P. Johnson, 1945–1992, was a leader in the Stonewall Rebellion of 1969.

CHAPTER 30

Gender expression and the imposition of a female/male dichotomy

In her book *Trans Liberation*, author, communist activist and transgender warrior Leslie Feinberg writes:

> We are a movement of masculine females and feminine males, crossdressers, transsexual men and women, intersexuals born on the anatomical sweep between female and male, gender-blenders, many other sex and gender-variant people, and our significant others. (5)

In this listing of gender-variant folk, and in the thousands of reports of sex and gender diversity found among the populations of the world's cultures, we find a type of human being and a manifestation of human culture unaddressed by the founders of Marxism.

Feinberg's important contribution to Marxist theory was to contextualize this part of the human family within the framework of the unfolding of the global class struggle. With convincing anthropological and historical evidence, she demonstrated how gender expression, like sexual expression, came to be manipulated, restricted and repressed by ruling-class forces with the onset of patriarchy.

In *Transgender Warriors*, a stunningly attractive book whose beautiful page layouts complement Feinberg's rich prose, she outlines her historical materialist analysis of gender expression, opening with a question:

> But did these cooperative [and hunting] societies only have room for two sexes, fixed at birth? It has become common for social scientists to conclude that the earliest human division of labor between women and men in communal societies formed the basis for modern sex and gender boundaries. But the more I studied, the more I believed that the assumption that every society, in every corner of the world, in every period of human history, recognized only men and women as two immutable social categories is a modern Western conclusion. …
>
> Our earliest ancestors do not appear to have been biological determinists. There are societies all over the world that allowed for more than two sexes, as well as respecting the right of individuals to reassign their sex. And transsexuality, transgender, intersexuality, and bigender appear as themes in creation stories, legends, parables, and oral history.
>
> As I've already documented, many Native nations on the North American continent made room for more than two sexes, and there appeared to have been a fluidity between them. Reports by military expeditions, missionaries, ethnographers, anthropologists, explorers, and other harbingers of colonialism cited numerous forms of sex-change, transgender, and intersexuality in matrilineal societies — societies where men were not in a dominant position. In these accounts — no matter how racist or angrily distorted by the colonial narrative voice — it is clear that transsexual priestesses and other trans spiritual leaders, or medicine people, have existed in many ancient cultures. (43-44)

'Gender and sex diversity are global in character'

In the following several pages, Feinberg provides examples of trans spiritual leaders in Asian, African and South American cultures. She concludes:

> I'm not arguing that all of these examples from diverse cultures are identical to modern Western trans identities. Nor am I trying to unravel the matrix of attitudes and beliefs around trans expression in these societies. The importance for me is the depth and breadth of evidence underscoring that gender and sex diversity are global in character, and that trans people were once revered, not reviled. How else could a trans person be a sacred shaman? In communal societies, where respect could not be bought or sold or stolen, being a shaman, or medicine person, was a position of honor. (47)

"So how and why," Feinberg asks, "did attitudes towards trans people plummet so drastically?" Guided by Engels, she finds the answer in the development of early class societies in the Middle Eastern Fertile Crescent. She remarks that, as a Jewish person, the anti-trans passages in Deuteronomy and the anti-homosexual passages in Leviticus bothered her. But they, like the campaigns against cross-dressing deities (e.g., the Syrian goddess Atargatis) and rulers (e.g., Egyptian Queen Hatshepsut and Assyrian King Ashurbanipal), were co-existent with the development of private property and the amassment of private wealth in the hands of men, as Engels so masterfully elucidates in *Origin*.

> Hostility to transgender, sex-change, intersexuality, women, and same-sex love became a pattern wherever class antagonisms deepened. As a Jewish, transgender, working-class revolutionary, I can't stress enough that Judaism was *not* the root of the oppression of women and the

> outlawing of trans expression and same-sex love. The rise
> of patriarchal class divisions were to blame.
>
> And I found that wherever the ruling classes became
> stronger, the laws grew increasingly more fierce and more
> relentlessly enforced. (Feinberg's italics; 53)

This writer would only caution that Judaism, like the other patriarchal religions of the world, has been a powerful ideological force since the overthrow of mother right and continues to be presently. The patriarchal religions exist most fundamentally as reflections of existing class relations, which, as Feinberg notes, are based on existing property relations: the private property relations of slave and feudal societies in the past, and presently, the global dominance of capitalist private property.

The existence of sex and gender variation among Indigenous people, especially among Native North American peoples, has received much attention, perhaps because of the stark division posed by their clear acceptance among tribal people in contrast to the prevalent homophobia and transphobia of capitalist society that is only now being challenged by a movement of the people who have been traditionally targeted and their allies.

Resolving an important issue involving word choice

Walter Williams' *The Spirit and the Flesh* offers a vast array of material highlighting the existence and importance of sex and gender-variant folk among Indigenous peoples. Criticism of his work by Native writers focuses on his uncritical use of the word "berdache," his importation of the word "amazon" to refer to both lesbian and two-spirit women in Indigenous cultures and his assumption that homosexuality was an essential ingredient of the berdache/amazon experience. These criticisms are raised by a number of the contributors to the book *Two-Spirit People*, most of whom, however, also acknowledge the trailblazing importance of Williams' research.

In the Preface to *Living the Spirit: A Gay American Indian Anthology*, Randy Burns of the Northern Paiute people and co-founder of Gay American Indians writes:

> French explorers used the word *berdache* to describe male Indians who specialized in the work of women and formed emotional and sexual relationships with other men. Many tribes had female berdaches, too — women who took on men's work and married other women. The History Project of Gay American Indians (GAI) has documented these alternative roles in over 135 North American tribes. ...
>
> As artists, providers, and healers, our traditional gay ancestors had important responsibilities.
>
> Women hunters and warriors brought food for their families and defended their communities, like the famous Kutenai woman warrior who became an intertribal courier and a prophet in the early 1800s, or Woman Chief of the Crow Indians, who achieved the third highest rank in her tribe. Among the Mohave [sic], lesbian women became powerful shamans and medicine people.
>
> Male berdaches specialized in the arts and crafts of their tribes and performed important social and religious roles. In California, we were often called upon to bury and mourn the dead, because such close contact with the spiritual world was considered too dangerous for others. Among the Navajo, berdaches were healers and artists, while among the Plains Indians, we were famous for the valuable crafts we made. (Roscoe 1988: Burns' italics; 1-2)

However, it's important to take seriously the controversy that has arisen over the use of the word "berdache." In the Introduction to the book *Two-Spirit People: Native*

American Gender Identity, Sexuality, and Spirituality, editors Sue-Ellen Jacobs, Wesley Thomas and Sabine Lang write:

> "Berdache" is now considered to be an inappropriate and insulting term by a number of Native Americans as well as by anthropologists. (3)

In its place:

> The term *two-spirit* (or *two-spirited*) was coined in 1990 by Native American individuals during the third Native American/First Nations gay and lesbian conference in Winnipeg. … Originating as a term for contemporary Native American gays and lesbians as well as people who have been referred to as "berdache" by anthropologists and other scholars, it has come to refer to a number of Native American roles and identities past and present, including contemporary Native Americans/First Nations individuals who are gay or lesbian; contemporary Native American/First Nations gender categories; the traditions wherein multiple gender categories and sexualities are institutionalized in Native American/First Nations tribal cultures; traditions of gender diversity in other, non-Native American cultures; transvestites, transsexuals, and transgendered people; and drag queens and butches. (the editors' italics; 2)

A relatively new term, an ancient concept

M. Tiahui, a Native activist and co-leader of United American Indians of New England, offered a very precise explanation of "Two Spirit" in her contribution to the 2019 Pride edition of ***Struggle-La Lucha*** newspaper:

> Perhaps you have heard the term "Two Spirit" used along with lesbian, gay, bisexual, transgender and other terms. If you are not Indigenous, this may have made you think that "Two Spirit" refers to Indigenous people who are lesbian, gay or bi. But being Two Spirit does not necessarily mean that someone is lesbian or gay since it does not refer to

sexual preference.

"Two Spirit" is a pan-Indian umbrella term that describes Indigenous people who have mixed or nonbinary gender roles. …

While the term is relatively new, the concept has existed among hundreds of Indigenous Nations for thousands of years. Some Native Nations have terms for up to 4 or 5 different genders, for instance. Two Spirit people are considered to be nonbinary and to hold sacred elements of both feminine and masculine within them. …

A Two Spirit person may be lesbian or gay, but being lesbian or gay does not necessarily make someone Two Spirit. …

Traditionally, in many tribal nations, Two Spirit people were held in high esteem. They were leaders, warriors, medicine (spiritual) people. They often played a special role with youth, including adopting children and giving special sacred names to babies. (2019: 2)

An encampment at the Standing Rock Indian Reservation during the 2016-2017 Native-led protests against the Dakota Access Pipeline.

Many people who have seriously considered the evidence, hold the opinion that LGBTQ2S, gender nonconforming, gender fluid and gender nonbinary folk have always been an essential part of the human family exactly because of the unique contributions they have made to our species' survival and well-being.

The present writer remembers, in a long past moment, reading a passage (but lacking memory of its source … a book? a journal article?) that highlights the crucial role that two-spirit people have played in Indigenous societies. The cited dialog between a young anthropologist and an elderly Native matriarch went something like this. The young investigator asks the woman, "Did there used to be special people in your tribe, people who married their own sex and perhaps dressed differently than other members of their gender?" The matriarch's face lights up. "Of course there were people like that. They were our problem solvers. They were the glue of our tribe."

CHAPTER 31

Peasant uprisings under feudalism

Most descriptions of "feudal society" focus on the historical period in Europe known as the Middle Ages (roughly A.D. 400 to 1500), although varying oppressive systems based on peasants tied to the land in the exploitative interests of landowners and tribute receivers existed, and still exist, in various other parts of the world, too. The serfs of Medieval Europe were exploited by feudal barons, who, in turn, had to pacify a king or higher-ranking noblemen. And the powerful Roman Catholic Church, owning at its peak fully one-third of Western Europe's land, also found ways to steal its share of the agricultural wealth generated by serf labor.

Engels writes in *Origin*:

> By the incessant civil wars and wars of conquest (the latter were particularly frequent under Charlemagne [A.D. 742-814]), the free land-owning peasants, the mass of the Frankish people, were reduced to the same state of exhaustion and penury as the Roman peasants in the last years of the Republic. ...
>
> Plundered and ruined by wars, they had been forced to put themselves under the protection of the new nobles or of the Church. ... But they had to pay dearly for it. Like the Gallic peasants earlier, they had to transfer their rights of property in land to their protecting lord and received the land back from him in tenancies of various and chang-

ing forms, but always only in return for services and dues. Once in this position of dependence, they gradually lost their personal freedom also; after a few generations most of them were already serfs. (213-214)

The commencement of European feudalism dates from the collapse of the Roman Empire and its slave-based economy. In *The German Ideology*, Marx and Engels offer an analysis:

> The third form of ownership is feudal or estate property. if antiquity started out from the *town* and its little territory, the Middle Ages started out from the *country*. This different starting point was determined by the sparseness of the population at that time, which was scattered over a large area and which received no large increase from the conquerors. In contrast to Greece and Rome, feudal development at the outset, therefore, extends over a much wider territory, prepared by the Roman conquests and the spread of agriculture at first associated with it. … The hierarchical structure of landownership, and the armed bodies of retainers associated with it, gave the nobility power over the serfs. (Engels' italics; 45)

'The mark' was a vestige of communalism

In previous chapters, we highlighted some of the negative aspects of the Agricultural Revolution. But in Engels' essay "The Mark" (Engels 1935b), we learn of a peasant-directed organization of agricultural land existent in many parts of Europe before and following the collapse of the Roman Empire that maintained vestiges of the communal property characteristic of preclass, communal society well into the epoch of feudalism.

The scope of "the mark" system included groups of farming villages and the associated shared land that the villagers used for cultivation and pasture, and the shared local water sources and forests. Also included in the concept were the popular assemblies of the peasants that determined how these resources were to be used.

With the passage of time, this widespread, agriculture-based system was undermined, with more and more poor peasants consigned to serfdom, until, all over Europe, what remained were mere small patches of land and forest designated "commons," whose resources were still available to the otherwise landless peasants. In the 1525 German Peasant War's manifesto, *The Twelve Articles of the Peasants*, a demand for the full restoration of the commons figured prominently, along with demands to reduce the amount of the "unseemly" tithe (a lifelong financial responsibility to the Church), an end to the treatment of peasants as property (serfdom!), an end to prohibitions of hunting and fishing and the collection of firewood on the part of the poor, no corvée (forced unpaid labor), fair rents, equal justice before the law and no heriot (a tax paid by the family when a family member died).

Engels describes the peasants' rebellions based on these demands in great detail in his book *The Peasant War in Germany.* He sets the scene:

> The urban society [of medieval Germany] was headed by the *patriciate*, the so-called *honourables*. They were the richest families. … They practiced usury in grain and money, seized monopolies of all kinds, gradually deprived the community of all rights to communal use of town forests and meadows and used them exclusively for their

own private benefit, exacted arbitrary road-, bridge- and gate-tolls and other imposts, and trafficked in trade, guild, and burgher privileges, and in justice. They treated the peasants of the town precincts with no more consideration than did the nobility and clergy. (Engels' italics; 7)

And further along he notes:

The common pastures and woods of the peasants were almost everywhere forcibly appropriated by the lords. The lord did as he pleased with the peasant's own person, his wife and daughters, just as he did with the peasant's property. He had the right of the first night. He threw the peasant into the tower when he wished, and the rack awaited the peasant there. … He killed the peasant or had him beheaded when he pleased.

The Inquisition unleashed its wrath on "sodomites."

Though gnashing their teeth under the terrible burden, the peasants were still difficult to rouse to revolt. They were scattered over large areas, and this made collusion between them extremely difficult. The old habit of submission inherited by generation from generation, lack of practice in the use of arms in many regions, and the varying degree of exploitation depending on the personality of the lord, all combined to keep the peasant quiet. For this reason we find so many local peasant insurrections in the Middle Ages but, prior to the Peasant War, not a single general national peasant revolt, at least in Germany. (10-11)

A movement too far ahead of its time

The leading figure in the Peasant War, according to Engels, was Thomas Münzer:

> As Münzer's religious philosophy approached atheism, so his political programme approached communism. (23)

He was a grassroots activist who traveled the highways and byways, agitating and articulating their grievances everywhere that there were peasants willing to listen. The resulting uprisings, culminating in 1525, were, however, according to Engels, foreordained to be unsuccessful given the existing class relations of that period.

Engels explains:

> Not only the movement of [Münzer's] time, but also the age, were not ripe for the ideas of which he himself had only a faint notion. The class which he represented was still in its birth throes. It was far from developed enough to assume leadership over, and to transform society. (71)

Münzer and other peasant leaders were captured and killed. In one of the battles:

> Out of 8,000 peasants, over 5,000 were slaughtered. (74)

Engels concludes:

> Those who suffered most from the Peasant War [besides the peasants themselves!] were the *clergy*. Their monasteries and endowments were burned, their treasuries plundered, sold abroad or melted down, and their stores consumed. …
>
> The *nobility* had also suffered considerably. Most of the noblemen's castles were destroyed and some of the most respected families were ruined. …
>
> The *towns*, too, generally gained nothing from the Peasant War. The rule of the honourables was almost everywhere re-established.
>
> Under the circumstances, the *princes* alone had benefited from the Peasant War. (Engels' italics; 80-81)

These brief excerpts from Engels' ***The Peasant War in Germany*** provide some background for the more geographically generalized and very remarkable contemporary analysis of this same period of class struggle in Europe that we'll learn about in the next chapter.

At this point, the reader may be wondering, "OK, an interesting manifestation of class struggle, but where were the women?" Keep reading!

CHAPTER 32

The war on women during the transition from feudalism to capitalism

We noted earlier the burdensome labor demands of the Agricultural Revolution, the introduction, for the first time, of private ownership of land and other resources, and the overthrow of "mother right," specifically, the enslavement of women (and children!) and later, of men. Feudal society has been characterized as a long period of social stagnation. But actually, there was an important force for change at work. Up to this point, we've neglected to mention a socioeconomic development of the feudal period that helped to lay the basis for capitalism: the growth of commodity production in the towns.

The early feudal economy in Europe was based on the local self-sufficiency of each feudal estate. The debt-burdened serf families labored part of the workweek producing food for themselves and part producing food for their lord and his family. But they also produced many other domestic life necessities for the manor such as cloth, tools, furniture, etc. This was production for use. In the towns, however, production for exchange, the production of commodities, was growing. Feminist scholar Silvia Federici, in her book-length analysis titled *Caliban and the Witch*, has much to say about the maturing of this important development in Europe in the 16th and 17th centuries, the so-called mercantilist era.

Federici's thesis is that the rise of capitalism in Europe in this period "demanded a genocidal attack on women" and that witch hunts were the principal means by which this attack was unleashed.

Proletarianized men, targeted women

Karl Marx, the heroic defender and promoter of the world's working class, was wont to remind workers that everything of value is produced by their labor. One could reasonably suppose, then, that with the advent of capitalist production, with its expand-or-die dynamic and lust for ever increasing private profit, more and more human resources, including women, would necessarily need to be conscripted into the working class. Yet Federici points out that while the proletarianization of peasant men proceeded apace in the towns, this was not the case with regard to women, quite the opposite.

She argues that as commercial relations, which originated in the towns, began penetrating the countryside, the position of serf women deteriorated and, according to Federici, as a result, a majority of the serfs who escaped the feudal estates for the towns and cities were women.

Also attracting women were the so-called heretical movements of the time:

> Heresy was as much a critique of social hierarchies and economic exploitation as it was a denunciation of clerical corruption. … The rejection of all forms of authority and a strong anti-commercial sentiment were common elements among the sects. (34)

Rejection of Catholic Church doctrine was another important feature of the heretical movements:

> From a very early period (after Christianity became a state religion in the 4th century), the clergy recognized the power that sexual desire gave women over men, and persistently tried to exorcize it by identifying holiness with avoidance of women and sex. Expelling women from any moment of the liturgy and from the administration of the sacraments; trying to usurp women's life-giving, magical powers by adopting a feminine dress; and making sexuality an object of shame -- all these were the means by which a patriarchal caste tried to break the power of women and erotic attraction. (37)

On the other hand:

> One of the most significant aspects of the heretical movement is the high status it assigned to women. ... In the church women were nothing but here they were considered equal: they had the same rights as men, and could enjoy a social life and mobility (wandering, preaching) that nowhere else was available to them in the Middle Ages. (38)
>
> We know ... that women did try to control their reproductive functions, as references to abortion and the use of contraceptives by women are numerous in the Penitentials [church rules governing confessions of sin]. (39)

But church attacks on the nonconformers were fierce and relentless:

> By the mid-14th century the Inquisitors' reports were no longer content with accusing the heretics of sodomy and sexual license. Now heretics were accused of animal worship ... and of indulging in orgiastic rituals, night flights and child sacrifices. (40)

A temporary increase in peasants' and workers' power

Federici spends many pages describing in detail the rebellions of serfs, day laborers and the poor of the towns under the influence of the heretical ideals of freedom and equality. But:

> A turning point in the course of the medieval struggles was the Black Death, which killed, on an average, between 30 percent and 40 percent of its population. … Coming in the wake of the Great Famine of 1315-1322, that weakened people's resistance to disease … this unprecedented demographic collapse profoundly changed Europe's social and political life. …
>
> The most important consequence of the plague was the intensification of the labor crisis generated by the class conflict; for the decimation of the work-force made labor extremely scarce, critically increased its cost, and stiffened people's determination to break the shackles of feudal rule. (44)
>
> For a broad section of the western European peasantry, and for urban workers, the 15th century was a period of unprecedented power. Not only did the scarcity of labor give them the upper hand, but the spectacle of employers competing for their services strengthened their sense of self-value, and erased centuries of degradation and subservience.
>
> However, by the end of the 15th century, a counter-revolution was already under way at every level of social and political life. (46-47)

Federici describes a virtual war against women, especially proletarian and poor women, unleashed by political authorities. Changes to the legal codes actually encouraged rape, and:

> The Church came to see prostitution as a legitimate activity. The state-managed brothel was believed to provide an antidote to the orgiastic sexual practices of

the heretic sects, and to be a remedy for sodomy, as well as a means to protect family life. (49)

'An enemy far more dangerous than the nobility'

Summarizing the character of the class struggle of this period of European history, Federici writes:

> By the late Middle Ages, wherever we turn, from Tuscany to England and the Low Countries, we find the bourgeoisie already allied with the nobility in the suppression of the lower classes. For in the peasants and the democratic weavers and cobblers of its cities, the bourgeoisie recognized an enemy far more dangerous than the nobility. (50)

Then, tackling the so-called transition to capitalism, she writes:

> As we know, "conquest, enslavement, robbery, murder, in brief force" [here citing words from Marx's description of the shift to capitalism in his book *Capital*] were the pillars of this process. ... Thus, the concept of a "transition to capitalism" is in many ways a fiction. (62)

The "primitive accumulation" of capital resources necessary for the establishment of the global capitalist economy was only attained through the enslavement of Africans, the genocide waged against other Indigenous peoples and the plundering of their lands' resources. Paralleling these atrocities, Federici notes the unfolding of an unprecedented "war" against women.

Federici elaborates:

> With the demise of the subsistence economy that had prevailed in pre-capitalist Europe, the unity of production and reproduction which has been typical of all societies based on production-for-use came to an end, as these activities became the carriers of different social relations

and were sexually differentiated. In the new monetary regime, only production-for-market was defined as a value-creating activity, whereas the reproduction of the worker began to be considered as valueless from an economic viewpoint and even ceased to be considered as work. … Women were excluded from many waged occupations and, when they worked for a wage, they earned a pittance compared to the average male wage. (74-75)

The witch hunt — an understudied phenomenon

Federici devotes much of her book to a description of the means by which the debasement of the social and economic status of women in Europe and beyond was carried out.

She places great emphasis on the employment of witch hunts in the effort to downgrade women:

The witch-hunt rarely appears in the history of the proletariat. To this day, it remains one of the most understudied phenomena in European history or, rather, world history, if we consider that the charge of devil worshipping was carried out by missionaries and conquistadors to the "New World" as a tool for the subjugation of the local population. (163)

The dimensions of the massacre should have raised some suspicions, as hundreds of thousands of women were burned, hanged, and tortured in less than two centuries. It should have also seemed significant that the witch-hunt occurred simultaneously with the colonization of the populations of the New World, the English enclosures, the beginning of the slave trade, the enactment of "bloody laws" against vagabonds and beggars, and it climaxed in that interregnum between the end of feudalism and the capitalist "takeoff" when the peasantry of Europe reached the peak of its power but, in time, also consummated its historic defeat. (164-165)

Graphic Zentralbibliothek, Zürich

Women being burned at the stake, drawing, 16th century.

Chastising historians for their lack of serious attention to this horrific campaign, she writes:

> [T]he unleashing of a campaign of terror against women, unmatched by any other persecution, weakened the resistance of the European peasantry to the assault launched against it by the gentry and the state, at a time when the peasant community was already disintegrating under the combined impact of land privatization, increased taxation, and the extension of state control over every aspect of social life. The witch-hunt deepened the divisions between women and men, teaching men to fear the power of women, and destroyed a universe of practices, beliefs, and social subjects whose existence was incompatible with the capitalist work discipline, thus redefining the main elements of social reproduction. (165)

Referencing the European peasant uprisings of the 16th and early 17th centuries, Federici writes:

> [I]n England, … hundreds of men, women and children, armed with pitchforks and spades, set about destroying the fences erected around the commons, proclaiming that "from now on we needn't work anymore." In France, in 1593-1595, there was the revolt of the Croquants against

the tithes, excessive taxation, and the rising price of bread, a phenomenon that caused mass starvation in large areas of Europe.

During these revolts, it was often women who initiated and led the action. Exemplary were the revolt that occurred at Montpellier in 1645, which was started by women who were seeking to protect their children from starvation, and the revolt at Cordoba in 1652 that likewise was initiated by women. It was women, moreover, who (after the revolts were crushed, with many men imprisoned or slaughtered) remained to carry on the resistance, although in a more subterranean manner. ...

The persecution of witches grew on this terrain. It was class war carried out by other means. (175-176)

Surviving records document a continent wide attack on urban women's economic status

Historian David Herlihy's book length collection of essays titled *Women, Family and Society in Medieval Europe* is divided into four parts. Part II, relying to a great extent on public records and documents of the time, focuses on the changing economic status of women in western Europe's medieval urban centers.

Early on in this section of the book, Herlihy writes:

About [A.D.] 965, an Arab geographer, Ibrahim ibn-lakub, described Slavic marriage customs, which, in many respects, were typical of all barbarian [sic] Europe. Ibrahim reported that the "marital price" required of grooms was so high that "if a man has two or three daughters, they are as riches to him; if, however, boys are born to him, this becomes for him a cause of poverty." Nearly the same complaint would be widely heard again in Europe during the late Middle Ages (1350-1500), but the sexual references would be exactly reversed. (60-61)

He's referring, of course, to the marriage-related reversal that we encountered earlier in this book: the historic switch, accompanying the overthrow of mother right, from bride price to dowry.

Herlihy continues:

> In the overwhelmingly rural world of the early Middle Ages, women enjoyed a high social value and entered marriage under favorable terms. But the bases of their preferment seem to have been the taxing physical labor they performed and the substantial contribution they made to the peasant household. With the growth and transformation of the medieval economy — and in particular the rise of towns from the twelfth century on — women's participation in the domestic economy grew restricted. Daughters no longer made a father rich and the terms under which they entered marriage turned against them. (67-68)

Using town and city censuses and other public records, Herlihy presents convincing evidence of the deep decline over time in the social and economic status of urban women. He concludes, following his presentation of mounds of evidence to the point:

> Women's participation in urban economic enterprises was reduced dramatically across the Middle Ages. In the thirteenth and early fourteenth centuries, women retained high visibility in a great variety of urban employments. They dominated some industries, such as the making of silk and linen cloths; in many other industries, they worked alongside men without apparent discrimination.
>
> The closing period of the Middle Ages, the fourteenth and fifteenth centuries, was a violent age of deep crises and difficult recovery; it also saw the end of this easy partnership between men and women in the urban economies. Guilds and governments, especially in the fifteenth century,

imposed severe restrictions on women's work. These restrictions amounted at times to the full exclusion of women from prestigious and well-paying jobs. (91)

Herlihy offers several possible explanatory factors that "merit thought and attention: urbanization, capitalization, the saturated markets of the medieval economy and monopolization." (92) But a bit forlornly, he concludes:

In the present state of knowledge, it is impossible to offer a truly rigorous explanation as to why women lost visibility in the urban economies between the thirteenth and the fifteenth or sixteenth centuries. (94-95)

It's interesting to note that Herlihy makes short shrift of the heretical movements and peasant and worker rebellions that challenged the patriarchal forces of church and state and offers only one brief allusion to "witchcraft":

[W]itchcraft, like mystical movements in orthodoxy, like heresy, swelled in strength in the late Middle Ages. The structure of late-medieval society may have restricted the access of women to property and office, but it could not silence or repress them. (56)

Unfortunately, though, in many ways, it did.

Professor Herlihy died in 1991, more than a decade before the appearance of Federici's book. In any case, he makes no mention at all of the horrific, continent wide (and beyond) witch hunt detailed by her. We think there are compelling reasons to believe that it was exactly the grave threat posed by a mass of rebellious and heretical women to the forces of patriarchal religion and emergent mercantile capitalism that led to their exclusion from public labor and their mass persecution.

CHAPTER 33

Engels' description of the economic dynamics of class society

The last chapter of Engels' *Origin* includes a description of the economics underlying the social/sexual evolution of class society:

> In conclusion, let us examine the general economic conditions which already undermined the gentile organization at the upper stage of barbarism [the full blossoming of the Agricultural Revolution] and with the coming of civilization [slavery! feudalism!] overthrew it completely. Here we shall need Marx's *Capital* as much as Morgan's book. (217)
>
> Wealth increased rapidly, but as the wealth of individuals. The products of weaving, metalwork and the other handicrafts, which were becoming more and more differentiated, displayed growing variety and skill. In addition to corn [the seeds of cereal grasses], leguminous plants and fruits, agriculture now provided wine and oil, the preparation of which had been learned. Such manifold activities were no longer within the scope of one and the same individual; *the second great division of labor* took place — handicraft separated from agriculture. ... Slavery, which during the preceding period was still in its beginnings and sporadic, now becomes an essential constituent part of the social system. ... With the splitting up of production into the two great main branches, agriculture and handicrafts,

arises production directly for exchange, commodity production. ...

The distinction of rich and poor appears beside that of freemen and slaves — with the new division of labor, a new cleavage of society into classes. The inequalities of property among the individual heads of families break up the old communal household communities wherever they had still managed to survive, and with them the common cultivation of the soil by and for these communities. The cultivated land is allotted for use to single families, at first temporarily, later permanently. The transition to full private property is gradually accomplished, parallel with the transition of the pairing marriage into monogamy. The single family is becoming the economic unit of society. (Engels' italics; 223)

Merchants, money, land as a commodity, and monogamy

[The development of productive forces] adds a third division of labor ... of decisive importance. It creates a class which no longer concerns itself with production, but only with the exchange of the products — *the merchants*. Under the pretext that they save the producers the trouble and risk of exchange, extend the sale of their products to distant markets and are therefore the most useful class of the population, a class of parasites comes into being ... who, as a reward for their actually very insignificant services, skim all the cream off production at home and abroad, rapidly amass enormous wealth and a corresponding social influence. ...

With the formation of the merchant class came also the development of *metallic money*, the minted coin, a new instrument for the domination of the non-producer over the producer and his production. The commodity of commodities had been discovered, that which holds all other commodities hidden in itself, the magic power which can change at will into everything desirable and desired. The man who had it ruled the world of production, and who had more of it than anybody else? — the merchant. … After commodities had begun to sell for money, loans and advances in money came also, and with them interest and usury. …

When the new landed proprietor shook off once and for all the fetters laid upon him by the prior right of gens [clan] and tribe, he also cut the ties which had hitherto inseparably attached him to the land. Money, invented at the same time as private property in land, showed him what that meant. Land could now become a commodity; it could be sold and pledged. Scarcely had private property in land been introduced than the mortgage was already invented. …

With trade expansion, money and usury, private property in land and mortgages, the concentration and centralization of wealth in the hands of a small class rapidly advanced, accompanied by an increasing impoverishment of the masses and an increasing mass of impoverishment. The new aristocracy of wealth, in so far as it had not been identical from the outset with the old hereditary aristocracy, pushed it permanently into the background. … And simultaneous with this division of the citizens into classes according to wealth, there was an enormous increase … in the number of slaves whose forced labor was the foundation on which the superstructure of the entire society was reared. (Engels' italics; 224-227)

With slavery … came the first great cleavage of society into an exploiting and an exploited class. … Slavery is the first form of exploitation, the form peculiar to the ancient world; it is succeeded by serfdom in the middle ages and wage labor in the more recent period. These are the three great forms of servitude characteristic of the three great epochs of civilization; open, and in recent times disguised, slavery always accompanies them. …

The form of family corresponding to civilization and coming to definite supremacy with it is monogamy, the domination of the man over the woman and the single family as the economic unit of society. The central link in civilized society is the state, which in all typical periods is without exception the state of the ruling class and in all cases continues to be essentially a machine for holding down the oppressed, exploited class. ...

With this as its basic constitution, civilization achieved things of which gentile [pre-class] society was not even remotely capable. But it achieved them by setting in motion the lowest instincts and passions in man and developing them at the expense of all his other abilities. From its first day to this, sheer greed was the driving spirit of civilization; wealth and again wealth and once more wealth, wealth, not of society but of the single scurvy individual — here was its one and final aim. (234-235)

Morgan's assessment of human social evolution

In homage to Lewis Henry Morgan, Engels concludes *Origin* with Morgan's words offering a general assessment of human social evolution:

Since the advent of civilization, the outgrowth of property has been so immense, its forms so diversified, its uses so expanding and its management so intelligent in the interests of its owners, that it has become, on the part of the people, an unmanageable power. *The human mind stands bewildered in the presence of its own creation.* The time will come, nevertheless, when human intelligence will rise to the mastery over property, and define the relations of the state to the property it protects, as well as the obligations and the limits of the rights of its owners. The interests of society are paramount to individual interests, and the two must be brought into just and harmonious relations. A mere property career is not the final destiny of mankind, if progress is to be the law of the future as it has been of the past. The time which has passed away since civilization began is but a fragment of the past duration of man's existence; and but a fragment of the ages yet to come. The dissolution of society bids fair to become the termination of a career of which property is the end and aim; because such a career contains the elements of self-destruction. Democracy in government, brotherhood in society, equality in rights and privileges, and universal education, foreshadow the next higher plane of society to which experience, intelligence and knowledge are steadily tending. *It will be a revival, in a higher form, of the liberty, equality and fraternity of the ancient gentes.* (Engels' italics; Morgan 1985: 552)

CHAPTER 34

Working-class marriage under capitalism

In setting the stage for an examination of working-class marriage in the epoch of capitalist society, the words of Karl Marx in his *Genesis of Capital* constitute a good introduction:

> The discovery of gold and silver in America, the extirpation, enslavement and entombment in mines of the aboriginal population, the beginning of the conquest and looting of the East Indies, the turning of Africa into a warren for the commercial hunting of black skins, signalised the rosy dawn of the era of capitalist production. (45)

Marx declared that:

> It was "the strange God" who perched himself on the altar cheek by jowl with the old Gods of Europe, and one fine day with a shove and a kick chucked them all of a heap. It proclaimed surplus-value making as the sole end and aim of humanity. (48)

By "surplus-value making," Marx was referring to the process of expropriation by which, under the capitalist system, most of the wealth produced by workers ends up in the pockets of the fat cats.

A complementary formulation appears in *The Communist Manifesto:*

> The modern bourgeois society that has sprouted from the ruins of feudal society has not done away with class

antagonisms. It has but established new classes, new conditions of oppression, new forms of struggle in place of the old ones. (Marx and Engels 1965: 31)

The ironies of 'legal equality' in marriage

Addressing the change in marriage relations that accompanied the transition to capitalism in Europe, Frederick Engels writes in *Origin*:

> So it came about that the rising bourgeoisie, especially in Protestant countries where existing conditions had been most severely shaken, increasingly recognized freedom of contract also in marriage. … Marriage remained class marriage, but within the class the partners were conceded a certain degree of freedom of choice. And on paper, in ethical theory and in poetic description, nothing was more immutably established than that every marriage is immoral which does not rest on mutual sexual love and really free agreement of husband and wife. …
>
> This human right, however, differed in one respect from all other so-called human rights. While the latter in practice remain restricted to the ruling class (the bourgeoisie) and are directly or indirectly curtailed for the oppressed class (the proletariat), in the case of the former the irony of history plays another of its tricks. The ruling class remains dominated by the familiar economic influences and therefore only in exceptional cases does it provide instances of really freely contracted marriages, while among the oppressed class … [freely contracted] marriages are the rule. (144)

Engels explains that it follows from this class distinction that:

> Sex love in the relationship with a woman becomes and can only become the real rule among the oppressed classes, which means today among the proletariat —

whether this relation is officially sanctioned or not. But here all the foundations of typical monogamy are cleared away. Here there is no property, for the preservation and inheritance of which monogamy and male supremacy were established: hence there is no incentive to make this male supremacy effective. …

Here quite other personal and social conditions decide. And now that large-scale industry has taken the wife out of the home onto the labor market and into the factory, and made her often the breadwinner of the family, no basis for any kind of male supremacy is left in the proletarian household, except, perhaps, for something of the brutality toward women that has spread since the introduction of monogamy. The proletarian family is therefore no longer monogamous in the strict sense, even where there is passionate love and firmest loyalty on both sides and maybe all the blessings of religious and civil authority.

Here, therefore, the eternal attendants of monogamy, hetaerism [sex work] and adultery, play only an almost vanishing part. The wife has in fact regained the right to dissolve the marriage, and if two people cannot get on with one another, they prefer to separate. In short, proletarian marriage is monogamous in the etymological sense of the word, but not at all in its historical sense. (135)

Social and economic inequality remain

Addressing the supposed equality between marriage partners brought into existence by the marriage contract, Engels observes:

Modern civilized systems of law increasingly acknowledge first, that for a marriage to be legal it must be a contract freely entered into by both partners and secondly, that also in the married state both partners must stand on a common footing of equal rights and duties. If both these demands are consistently carried out, say the jurists, women have all they can ask. (135-136)

In the great majority of cases today, at least in the possessing classes, the husband is obligated to earn a living and support his family, and that in itself gives him a position of supremacy without any need for special legal titles and privileges. Within the family he is the bourgeois, and the wife represents the proletariat. (137)

Citing and continuing Engels' train of thought, Dorothy Ballan, in *Feminism and Marxism*, writes:

Engels reminds us that when the monogamous family household lost its public character, it no longer concerned society. It became a private service, and the wife became the head servant excluded from all social production. Only large-scale industry has opened social production to the proletarian wife.

"But," [Engels] says, "it was opened in such a manner that if she carries out her duties in the private service for her family, she remains excluded from public production and unable to earn; and if she wants to take part in public production and earn independently, she cannot carry out family duties. The wife's position in the factory is similar to the position of women in all branches of business right up to medicine and the law. The modern individual family is founded on the open or concealed domestic slavery of the wife, and modern society is a mass composed of these individual families as its molecules." (29)

Citing the viewpoint of Marxist theorist and revolutionary V.I. Lenin, Ballan continues:

On this very question, Lenin, after the Russian revolution, had this to say: "Notwithstanding all the liberating laws that have been passed, woman continues to be a domestic slave, because petty housework crushes, strangles, stultifies and degrades her, chains her to the kitchen and to the nursery, and wastes her labor on *barbarously unproductive,* petty, nervewracking, stultifying and crushing drudgery. The real emancipation of women … will begin only when a mass struggle is started against this petty domestic economy, or rather when it is transformed on a mass scale into large-scale socialist economy." (Ballan's italics; 29)

Further on in *Feminism and Marxism* Ballan writes:

The millennia of women's oppression began, as Engels said, when women were excluded from participation in public life, industry and economic life generally, and were reduced to the pettiness and drudgery of individual private work.

Today, in the space age, the last vestiges of the crude division of labor, whereby the woman is relegated to the semi-slavery of household chores and the man participates and dominates all other phases of social life, are crumbling. …

As Marx said, when the production relations of a given society are no longer compatible with the social relations, which really belong to a previous epoch, "the social relations burst asunder" — then comes a period of revolution, first of all in the consciousness of the oppressed. (57)

Woman warrior, Fallen Leaf.

CHAPTER 35

Indigenous sisters inspire colonial settler sisters to fight misogyny

An excerpt from the "Introduction" page of Sally Roesch Wagner's *Sisters in Spirit: Haudenosaunee (Iroquois) Influence on Early American Feminists* reads:

> We Haudenosaunee live within the traditional structure that we've always had, the structure of equality among all members of our community. Women, men, and children have equal spiritual, human, and political rights. We have equal opportunity to voice opinions or objections to any situation within our community, and we know our voice will be heard.
>
> And so, when we met these white women so long ago, I am sure that our women were probably shocked at the lack of human equality that these other women had to live under. And we, seeing them as equal — all women as equal — couldn't understand how not only women, but women and children, were living under this totally oppressive situation. How people who had fled their homelands, for exactly the same reason, could appear here on our Turtle Island, our Mother Earth, and bring with them the exact same oppressive behaviors that they had experienced. For the men to walk, set foot on this land and say, "This is mine, I want this, I'm taking this," is an example of how they were thinking. (signed) Jeanne Shenandoab, Onondaga Nation (10)

Sisters in Spirit tells the previously hidden history of how it was the inspiration and knowledge derived from contact with Indigenous women that drove white women activists of the colonial settler nation of the United States to fight for the previously unthinkable: equal rights with men!

Noting that, among the women's rights leaders of the mid nineteenth century, Matilda Joslyn Gage is less well known than some other leaders, such as Elizabeth Cady Stanton and Susan B. Anthony, for example, Wagner wants to make sure that Gage's contributions are recognized alongside those of other leaders:

> Gage wrote extensively about the Haudenosaunee, especially the position of women in what she termed their "matriarchate" or system of "mother-rule." She was working on a book about the Haudenosaunee when she died in 1898. In 1875, while president of the National Woman Suffrage Association, Gage wrote a series of newspaper articles on the Haudenosaunee. (28)

Wagner quotes Gage to show her deep understanding of the Native right to sovereignty:

> "Our Indians are in reality foreign powers, though living among us. With them our country not only has treaty obligations, but pays them, or professes to, annual sums in consideration of such treaties. … Compelling them to become citizens would be like the forcible annexation of Cuba, Mexico, or Canada to our government, and as unjust." (29)

A feminist calls for revolution

Gage held an astonishingly radical feminist viewpoint. Wagner cites her revolutionary political perspective:

"During the ages, no rebellion has been of like importance with that of Woman against the tyranny of Church and State; none has had its far-reaching effects. We note its beginning; its progress will overthrow every existing form of these institutions; its end will be a regenerated world." (40)

Offering background on Native-EuroAmerican relations of the period, Wagner writes:

Even though they lived in very different cultural, economic, spiritual, and political worlds during the early 1800s, EuroAmerican settlers in Central/Western New York were, at most, one person away from direct familiarity with Iroquois people. The Haudenosaunee continued their ancient practice of adopting individuals of other nations, and many white residents of New York (including Matilda Joslyn Gage) carried adoptive Indian names. Friendships and visiting were commonplace activities between Natives and non-Natives. ... These three leaders of the women's rights movement — Stanton, Gage, and [Lucretia] Mott — were among those who had a personal connection with the Haudenosaunee. (32)

Wagner confesses to having been a student of the early settler women's rights activists early on but hounded by a difficult question:

I could not fathom how they dared to dream their revolutionary dream. Living under the ideological hegemony of nineteenth-century United States, these women had no say in government, religion, economics, or social life. Whatever made them think that human harmony, respect for women's lives, and equal rights for women were achievable? Surely these white women, living under conditions they likened to slavery, did not receive their vision in a vacuum. (37)

Several pages further on, she provides a succinct answer:

> They believed women's liberation was possible because they knew liberated women, women who possessed rights beyond their wildest imagination: Haudenosaunee women. (41)

Wagner describes Mott's transformative experience:

> During the summer of 1848 the Motts visited Cattaraugus [a Native community in western New York state] where they witnessed women exercising equal authority in discussion and decision-making while the Seneca nation changed its governmental structure. Lucretia watched as the Native women planned the strawberry ceremony in a most non-Christian tradition of women's spiritual leadership. With her feminist vision fired by her first-hand experience of women's political, spiritual, social, and economic authority, Mott traveled from the Seneca nation to nearby Seneca Falls, where she and Stanton called the first women's rights convention in July. (44)

'Rape didn't exist among Native nations'

> Newspaper readers in New York … read interviews with white teachers who worked at various Indian nations testifying to the wonderful sense of freedom and safety they felt, since Indian men did not rape women. (44)
>
> Native men's intolerance of rape was commented on by many eighteenth and nineteenth century Indians and non-Indian reporters alike, many of whom contended that rape didn't exist among Native nations prior to white contact. (66)
>
> No utopian dream, body right was a birthright of Haudenosaunee women. Family lineage traditionally was reckoned through mothers; no child was born a "bastard" (the concept didn't exist). Every child found a loving and welcome place in a mother's world, surrounded by a mother's sisters, her mother, and the men whom they married. Unmarried sons and brothers lived in this large

extended family, too, until they left home to marry into another matrilineal clan. (48)

In 1794, at the last general council held by the U.S. government with the Iroquois Confederacy:

> Haudenosaunee women countered a prayer offered by Jemima Wilkinson, the itinerant preacher, who called on the Indians to repent. The Iroquois women responded through their representative that "the white people had pressed and squeezed them together, until it gave them great pain in their hearts, and they thought the white people ought to give back all the lands they had taken from them." They, in turn, called on the white people "to repent and wrong the Indians no more." (92)

Here are some snatches from the two-page chart (30-31) comparing — actually contrasting — the Haudenosaunee and EuroAmerican cultures of the 1800s:

> Children are members of the mother's clan vs. Children are the sole property of fathers; Violence against women not part of culture, and dealt with seriously when occurs vs. Husbands have legal right and religious responsibility to physically discipline wives; Work satisfying, done communally vs. Work drudgery, isolated; Work done under the direction of the women, working together vs. Work done under authority of the husband; Each woman controls her own personal property vs. No rights to her own property, body, or children; Women have responsibilities in [religious] ceremony vs. Women forbidden to speak in churches; Women choose their chief vs. Illegal for women to vote; Women hold key political offices (e.g., clan mothers) vs. Women excluded from political office; and Decision making by consensus, everyone has a vote vs. Decision making by men, majority rules.

We've tried to capture the gist of this amazing book in the foregoing paragraphs. But *Sisters in Spirit* has much more to offer.

The next chapter will further explore the views of V.I. Lenin and those of other Marxists on the institution of marriage and revolutionary efforts to free women from the historic scourge of patriarchal tyranny.

CHAPTER 36

Marriage and the struggle for socialism

evolution is necessary ... not only because the "ruling" class cannot be overthrown in any other way, but also because the class "overthrowing" it can only in a revolution succeed in ridding itself of all the muck of ages and become fitted to found society anew. (95)

This critically important formulation by Karl Marx and Frederick Engels is found in their co-authored work, *The German Ideology*. Certainly, "the muck of ages" must include the oppression of women and LGBTQ2S folk.

In the concluding section of *Feminism and Marxism*, Dorothy Ballan notes the advances in social/sexual relations brought about by the Bolshevik revolution of 1917:

> Its rich experience in the initial stages of the revolution still offers some of the most illuminating insights on what the starting point of the sexual revolution is, and how it was conceived by its leaders as part of the great socialist transformation of humanity. (60)

> The Bolsheviks began a new world historic process of dissolving the millennia of patriarchal society founded on private property, and began to construct a socialist cooperative society, free from patriarchal domination. It actually began to dismantle the patriarchy. What could be more significant for women? (62)

Alexandra Kollontai (1872-1952) was a Bolshevik Party member and a leader in the revolutionary Soviet government. In her contribution to a collection of essays eulogizing V.I. Lenin, she wrote:

> Vladimir Ilyich [Lenin] was the one who initiated the involvement of broad masses of women from the cities and villages in the building of a socialist state. … Not only the women of the Soviet Union, but women throughout the world should know that Vladimir Ilyich laid the foundations of female emancipation. … Nowhere in the world, nowhere in history is there such a thinker and statesman who has done so much for the emancipation of women as Vladimir Ilyich. (tinyurl.com/lllyrur)

V.I. Lenin's views on dismantling the patriarchy

In *The Emancipation of Women*, a book-length collection of the writings of Lenin on this crucial issue, we find the words:

> In the course of two years of Soviet power in one of the most backward countries of Europe more has been done to emancipate woman, to make her the equal of the "strong" sex, than has been done during the past 130 years by all the advanced, enlightened, "democratic" republics of the world taken together.
>
> Education, culture, civilization, freedom — all these high-sounding words are accompanied in all the capitalist, bourgeois republics of the world by incredibly foul, disgustingly vile, bestially crude laws that make women unequal in marriage and divorce, that make the child born out of wedlock and the "legally born" child unequal, and that give privileges to the male and humiliate and degrade womankind. (75)

But Lenin tempered his approval of the progress that had been so far achieved by the Soviets in the early days of the revolution by pointing out what still needed to be done:

Public catering establishments, nurseries, kindergartens — here we have examples of … the simple, everyday means, involving nothing pompous, grandiloquent or ceremonial, which can "really emancipate women," really lessen and abolish their inequality with men as regards their role in social production and public life.

These means are not new, they (like all the material prerequisites for socialism) were created by large-scale capitalism. But under capitalism they remained, first, a rarity, and secondly — which is particularly important — either "profit-making" enterprises, with all the worst features of speculation, profiteering, cheating and fraud, or "acrobatics of bourgeois charity," which the best workers rightly hated and despised. (64)

Lenin's discussions with Clara Zetkin

Starting in the autumn of 1920, Lenin held a series of discussions with Clara Zetkin, a founder and leader of the German Communist Party. Zetkin's notes on those discussions are reprinted in *The Emancipation of Women*. Lenin raised his concerns with Zetkin about the need for the full liberation of all women from the tyranny of patriarchy. As

Rosa Luxemburg and Clara Zetkin
in Mannheim, Germany, 1910

the great internationalist that he was, the global struggle against capitalism was always on his mind:

> We do not yet have an international Communist women's movement and we must have one without fail. We must immediately set about starting it. Without such a movement, the work of our International and of its parties is incomplete and never will be complete. (98)

In the matter of social/sexual relations, Lenin queried Zetkin at length on what he considered an overemphasis on personal sexuality and marriage problems at meetings of German working-class women and among the youth. Zetkin responded eloquently to Lenin's concern, emphasizing the use of historical materialist analysis in these discussions:

> Where private property and the bourgeois social order prevail [e.g., in Germany], questions of sex and marriage gave rise to manifold problems, conflicts and suffering for women of all social classes and strata. …
>
> Knowledge of the modifications of the forms of marriage and family that took place in the course of history, and of their dependence on economics, would serve to rid the minds of working women of their preconceived idea of the eternity of bourgeois society. The critically historical attitude to this had to lead to an unrelenting analysis of bourgeois society, an exposure of its essence and its consequences, including the branding of false sex morality. … Every truly Marxist analysis of an important part of the ideological superstructure of society, of an outstanding social phenomenon, had to lead to an analysis of bourgeois society and its foundation, private property. (102)

But Lenin needed more convincing:

> Can you assure me in all sincerity that during those reading and discussion evenings, questions of sex and marriage are dealt with from the point of view of mature, vital historical materialism? This presupposes wide-

ranging, profound knowledge, and the fullest Marxist mastery of a vast amount of material. (102)

This back and forth between Lenin and Zetkin continued, broaching a number of related issues. Lenin sought to clarify his position with the following words:

> Not that I want my criticism to breed asceticism. That is farthest from my thoughts. Communism should not bring asceticism, but joy and strength, stemming, among other things, from a consummate love life. Whereas today, in my opinion, the obtaining plethora of sex life yields neither joy nor strength. On the contrary, it impairs them. (107)

Leon Trotsky on the backtracking following Lenin's death

Leon Trotsky, who stood with Lenin in the front ranks of the Bolshevik revolution, expressed concerns similar to those of Lenin with regard to freeing women from domestic drudgery:

Vladimir Lenin giving a speech to the Red Army in Sverdlov Square, Moscow, May 5, 1920. On the right of the platform is Leon Trotsky, commander of the Red Army.

> Washing must be done by a public laundry, catering by a public restaurant, sewing by a public workshop. Children must be educated by good public teachers who have a real vocation for the work. Then the bond between husband and wife would be freed from everything external and accidental, and the one would cease to absorb the life of the other. Genuine equality would at last be established. (Trotsky 1973: 42)

Defeating the capitalists and feudalists through proletarian revolution in one of the world's poorest countries, and then struggling through civil war and imperialist invasion, the Soviets were, in the early days of the revolution, hard pressed to provide all that was materially required. Gradually though, through rational, socialist planning and the revolutionary dedication of the workers and peasantry, great strides forward that would have been impossible under capitalist rule were made. Politically, however, after the death of Lenin in January 1924, much was lost, as documented in great detail in Trotsky's later writings.

Having been forced into exile, in 1936 Trotsky wrote disparagingly of the backtracking of the privileged Stalinist bureaucracy on social/sexual matters as on other issues:

> The marriage and family laws established by the October Revolution, once the object of its legitimate pride, are being made over and mutilated by vast borrowings from the law treasuries of the bourgeois countries. And as though on

Jiang Qing

Nidia Díaz

> purpose to stamp treachery with ridicule, the same arguments which were earlier advanced in favor of unconditional freedom of divorce and abortion — "the liberation of women," "defense of the rights of personality," "protection of motherhood" — are repeated now in favor of their limitation and complete prohibition. (Trotsky 1973: 86-87)

Nonetheless, the Soviet Union, having come into existence bearing a millstone of millions of illiterate and desperately poor people, was, within a short period of time, able to produce several generations of socially secure, educated women, including many women in positions of authority and leadership. And the socialist goal to free women from patriarchal slavery has continued and grown in the century since the birth of the Soviet Union.

Socialist and communist leaders like Rosa Luxemburg in Germany, Nguyen Thi Binh (Madam Binh) in Vietnam, Jiang Qing (Chiang Ching) in China, Lolita Lebrón in Puerto Rico, Leila Khaled in Palestine, Nidia Díaz in El Salvador, Haydée Santamaría in Cuba, Titina Silla in Guinea Bissau, the Black Panther women in the U.S. and countless other revolutionary women have been an inspiration to millions, women and men alike, all around the world.

The next chapter will cite the gains in social/sexual relations made by the Cuban revolution.

Madame Nguyen Thi Binh in the Vietnam's National Liberation Front delegation to the Paris peace talks. London, 1969

LUCIA
☆ UN FILM CUBANO DE HUMBERTO SOLAS ☆
CON RAQUEL REVUELTA ☆ ESLINDA NUÑEZ ☆ ADELA LEGRA
☆ EDUARDO MOURE ☆ ADOLFO LLAURADO ☆

CHAPTER 37

Cuban women and Cuban marriage

With a bleeding eye in their hands, a sergeant and several other men went to the cell where our compañeras Melba Hernández and Haydée Santamaría were held. Addressing the latter, and showing her the eye, they said: "This eye belonged to your brother. If you will not tell us what he refused to say, we will tear out the other."

Haydée, who loved her valiant brother above all else, replied full of dignity: "If you tore out an eye and he did not speak, much less will I."

Later they came back and burned the women prisoners' arms with cigarettes until at last, full of malice, they told the young Haydée Santamaría: "You no longer have a fiancé because we've killed him too." But still imperturbable, she answered: "He is not dead, because to die for one's country is to live forever." Never had the heroism and the dignity of Cuban womanhood reached such heights. (Deutschmann and Shnookal 2007: 81)

The foregoing passage is from *History Will Absolve Me,* a translated transcript of the statement made by Fidel Castro at his 1953 trial in the kangaroo court of U.S.-supported Cuban tyrant Fulgencio Batista.

Melba Hernández and Haydée Santamaría

One of the first initiatives of the revolutionary government that took power in Cuba on Jan. 1, 1959, was the formation, in 1960, of the Federation of Cuban Women (Federación de Mujeres Cubanas) under the leadership of Sierra Maestra fighter Vilma Espín. Among the initial goals of the FMC, described by Colette Harris in her essay "Socialist Societies and the Emancipation of Women: The Case of Cuba," (1995: 91-113) were to create conditions allowing women full participation in the economy, to change the patterns of living in rural areas that contributed to the oppression of women, to provide social services to replace conditions of do-

Vilma Espín

mestic servitude, to equalize opportunities that previously favored men, to encourage women to take roles in political work and government, and to implement workplace changes addressing the particular needs of women in general and of mothers in particular.

The FMC at that time played a pivotal role in the revolution's campaign to eradicate illiteracy in Cuba. Ninety-one thousand women were mobilized in this unprecedented effort to empower the country's most oppressed by teaching them how to read and write. Seeking potential students in every corner of the island nation, the campaign was able to announce that by the end of 1961, universal literacy to the third-grade level had been achieved.

Among its many inspiring qualities, the Cuban revolution is known for its forthrightness and honesty. The Cuban film *Lucía*, released in 1968, offers three portraits of Cuban women: the stultifying life of a "privileged" woman under Spanish colonialism; the perilous struggle of a union organizer in the pre-revolutionary period of U.S.-controlled puppet governments; and the new challenges faced by a post-revolutionary Lucía.

In this third portrait, set in the context of the revolutionary government's literacy campaign, Lucía is taught to read and write by a young education volunteer who comes to her rural home. She is happily married, but her husband is conflicted by this new development. He clearly loves Lucía and wants the best for her, but he is also strongly possessive. He feels threatened by the time she spends with the young teacher and unsettled by the fact that her growing literacy is lessening her dependency on him.

There is no objective threat to their relationship, but the film ends as they engage in a lovers' quarrel on the beach near their home. In the film's last frames, the camera pans from the couple at the shoreline to the top of a sand dune where a girl (Lucía number four?) watches them fight and smiles. No, the film acknowledges, the defeat of the vestiges of patriarchy will not be accomplished in one generation. But it will be accomplished by the fundamental change brought about by a rational, planned economy that puts the needs of the people first and foremost. And the revolutionary will and effort personified by the Cuban revolution and the Cuban women and men in motion are a guarantee for continuing progress.

'The revolution within the revolution'

At the Fifth National Plenary of the FMC in 1966, Fidel Castro opened his remarks with the following words:

Arriving here this evening, I commented to a comrade that this phenomenon of women's participation in the revolution was a revolution within a revolution. … And if we were asked what the most revolutionary thing is that the revolution is doing, we would answer that it is precisely this — the revolution that is occurring among the women of our country! …

If we were asked what things in the revolution have been most instructive for us, we would answer that one of the most interesting lessons for revolutionaries is that being offered by our women. (Stone 1981: 64)

In that speech, Fidel alluded to the domestic enslavement of women and called for the mobilization of 1 million women to join the productive workforce of the country. Demonstrating the depth and seriousness of his thinking on this matter, he elaborated on the challenge:

Why can't this goal be reached in four years? Because in order to have one million women working in production, we must have thousands of children's day nurseries, thousands of primary boarding schools, thousands of school dining halls, thousands of workers' dining halls; thousands of centers of social services of this type must be set up. …

In order to reach the social goal of liberating women from all these activities that enslave her and impede her from full incorporation into work outside the home and all these activities in which she can engage in society, it is necessary to create the necessary material base, to attain the necessary social development. (70-71)

The Cuban Family Code

Along with the effort to provide a material basis for women to enter the public workforce, a new legislation-based initiative, with mass input and support, was undertaken.

On the verso of the cover of the official translation of the Cuban Family Code, provided by the New York City-based Center for Cuban Studies, we find this introduction:

> Following its discussion by the people and approval by more than 98 percent of the participants in the meetings and assemblies, the Family Code went into effect on March 8, International Women's Day, 1975, by virtue of a Law enacted by the Council of Ministers on February 14, 1975. Cubans are taking the provisions of the Family Code seriously, and the Code is helping to create one of the most basic conditions for further development of the Revolution, that of equality between men and women in all areas of Cuban life.

What are some of the provisions of that legislation? The code mandates equal rights and responsibilities for both marriage partners in the home. In general, "common law" marriages have equal legal standing with "legally formalized marriages." Article 26 reads:

> Both partners must care for the family they have created and each must cooperate with the other in the education, upbringing and guidance of the children according to the principles of socialist morality. They must participate, to the extent of their capacity or possibilities, in the running of the home, and cooperate so that it will develop in the best possible way. (8)

And Article 27 elaborates:

> However, if one of them only contributes by working at home and caring for the children, the other partner must contribute [financial] support alone, without prejudice to his duty of cooperating in the above mentioned work and care. (8)

In other words, his financial support of the family does not, in any respect, free the spouse from his responsibility to share in housework.

Under the code, children are guaranteed equal legal status, whether they are the dependents of biological parents, a single parent or an adopting guardian. Under Article 51 of the code, divorce is a simple matter:

> Divorce will take effect by common agreement or when the court determines that there are factors which have led the marriage to lose its meaning for the partners and for the children and, thus, for society as a whole. (12)

What have followed from the directives of the code are practical and important measures to ease the burdens of women working outside the home, including priority in the purchase of labor-saving appliances, help with grocery shopping (Plan Jaba), workplace cafeterias, extended hours beyond regular working hours at health clinics and other social services.

In her address to the 63rd Session of the United Nations Commission on the Status of Women in March 2019, Teresa Amarelle Boué, secretary general of Cuba's FMC and member of the Council of the State of the Republic of Cuba, delineated some of Cuba's achievements in the area of women's rights:

> The new Constitution of the Republic explicitly reaffirms the principle of equality and non-discrimination, guarantees and upholds human rights in accordance with the current reality and the national transformations that have been taking place. It further ensures that women can exercise their sexual and reproductive rights, protects them from violence in all its manifestations and spaces, and creates the institutional and legal mechanisms for this purpose, thereby reinforcing the State's express commitment to the principle of gender equality. ...
>
> The first social protection for Cuban women and men is to be guaranteed a decent job. Women represent 49 percent

of the labor force in the civil state sector and 34 percent of
the self-employed sector. …

Universal and free education — the right of all persons
— is a strategic foundation for promoting the participation
and empowerment of women and girls, as well as advanc-
ing in the eradication of prejudice and all types of discrimination and violence.

The presence of women in education is greater than that
of men. With respect to university enrollment, 65 percent
are women, representing 53.7 percent of graduates from
natural sciences and mathematics, and 66.9 percent of
graduates from medical sciences. Women also constitute 66
percent of higher education teaching staff and make up 48
percent of the scientific sector.

The promotion of women to managerial positions has
experienced a sustained growth of 50 percent of posts. In
addition, women make up 53.22 percent of Parliament and
hold two of the three highest ranking positions of this
body. They also constitute 48.4 percent of the State Council
and 33 percent are women ministers. They represent 78
percent of prosecutors and 77.5 percent of professional
judges. (misiones.minrex.gob.cu)

'Marriage' in revolutionary Cuba

The commitment of the Cuban revolution to the liberation of women, to their full participation in society, has
been a continuing, unwavering one, even in the face of the
extremely harmful and criminal U.S. blockade and the difficult "special period" occasioned by the collapse of the Soviet Union, previously Cuba's main trading partner.

The issue of full rights for lesbian, gay, bisexual, transgender and intersex people has received close attention in
Cuba. Unlike in the U.S., where powerful, right-wing religious forces (including both fundamentalist preachers and

the Catholic Church), capitalist billionaires and their political stooges continue to actively conspire to derail what advances have been won, in Cuba the issue is seen as a matter of mass consciousness raising. LGBTI Cubans themselves have a unique perspective on same-sex marriage.

Mariela Castro Espín is the director of the Cuban National Center for Sex Education (CENESEX) and a member of the Cuban Parliament (Asamblea Nacional del Poder Popular de Cuba). She is also a niece of Fidel Castro, and daughter of past Cuban President Raúl Castro and revolutionary leader Vilma Espín. She is well-known globally for her strong and consistent advocacy for LGBTI Cubans. During an interview with the French news agency AFP in 2013, parts of which were reprinted on the *El Nuevo Herald* webpage, she explained how the issue of same-sex marriage is viewed by many of those directly affected:

> What the vast majority of gay and lesbian people raise is that they are interested in the legalization of consensual unions to have inheritance rights. That is what really affects them, because in Cuba the majority of straight people do not get married. It's not a priority. (elnuevoherald.com, Aug. 16, 2013. Translation by the present author)

During the nationwide, monthslong discussion of the proposed new Cuban Constitution before the referendum itself, which took place on Feb. 24, 2019, it became clear that a majority of Cubans were not yet ready to support a clause extending marriage rights to same-sex couples. However, Watermark Online daily news service quoted prominent gay Cuban blogger Francisco Rodríguez Cruz (aka Paquito de Cuba) as noting that the new constitution "expressly prohibits and punishes [anti-LGBTI discrimination] under law" and recognizes "the right of all people to form a family and protects all families." (www.watermarkonline.com) And CENESEX has emphasized that it will continue the struggle, focusing on making a change to the Cuban Family Code that will extend marriage rights to same-sex couples.

A fair assessment of revolutionary Cuba's progress on the issues affecting LGBTI folk must acknowledge that the revolution did not instill homophobia and transphobia into Cuban culture. No, this was the historic legacy of the Roman Catholic Church and Spanish imperialism, compounded in the 20th century by U.S. imperialist domination until the victorious revolution of 1959. And following that victory, it must always be taken into account that Cuba has been the constant target of U.S. hostile propaganda and actions, most infamously, the economic blockade, but also including numerous acts of CIA-directed sabotage and CIA efforts to assassinate Cuban leaders. In other words, revolutionary Cuba has been forced to develop, throughout its decades long history, under constant, near warlike conditions.

Defending trans lives: a tale of two systems

Despite these difficult circumstances, one need only compare the status of trans people in Cuba with their status in the U.S., to appreciate the superiority of Cuba's socialist system. Revolutionary Cuba has no history of anti-transgender violence. And since 2010, the Cuban government has provided sex reassignment surgery free of charge as part of their widely praised free universal health care system. In the U.S., murderous attacks on transgender people, especially trans women of color, are commonplace. And the inaccessibility of any quality health care for millions of poor people in the U.S., especially people of color, continues to be a criminal outrage.

Another indication of the vast gulf that separates Cuba's approach to LGBT issues from that of the U.S. is the diametrically different response of the two countries to the AIDS crisis of the 1980s and beyond. Transgender warrior Leslie Feinberg, in her book, ***Rainbow Solidarity in Defense of Cuba***, which is both a brief political history of Cuba as well as a heartfelt act of firm solidarity with the socialist island, describes in detail the Cuban government's scientific and humane approach to the epidemic in contrast to the homophobic, genocidal program of inaction demonstrated by the U.S. government:

> In the U.S., AIDS was first diagnosed in 1981. By May 2, 1983, simultaneous gay and lesbian protests of tens of thousands had to take to the streets in New York City, San Francisco, Los Angeles, Houston, Atlanta, Chicago and Milwaukee under banners reading, "Fighting for our lives!" to demand federal funds to battle AIDS, and for research, services and Social Security benefits. ...
>
> The president [Ronald Reagan] had still not publicly said the word AIDS, while theo-cons [theological conservatives] demonized the emerging health crisis as a "gay plague." ...
>
> By contrast, Cuba's health care workers began preparations to defend the whole population from the AIDS epidemic two years before the first case was diagnosed on the island in 1985. Cuba spared no expense despite the chokehold of the U.S.-led blockade.
>
> Cuba — unlike the U.S. — mobilized against AIDS, not against people with AIDS. (2009: 45)

CHAPTER 38

Women and revolution

"As we come marching, marching, we bring the greater days. The rising of the women means the rising of the race. No more the drudge and idler — ten that toil where one reposes. But a sharing of life's glories: Bread and roses, bread and roses."

In 1912, the women textile workers of Lawrence, Mass., went out on strike. Their demands were most eloquently expressed in banners proclaiming "Bread and Roses." These two objectives were first linked in a 1911 speech by women's suffrage campaigner Helen M. Todd. Subsequently, they inspired a poem by James Oppenheim that was then set to music by Martha Coleman. (folkarchive.de/breadrose.html)

At a time when reactionary attacks against women's reproductive rights are gaining momentum across the U.S., this work has been an effort to step back and examine, from a historical (and prehistoric) materialist perspective, the evolution of the status of women both within and apart from the institution of "marriage."

A historical materialist approach, first consistently applied to human social evolution by Karl Marx and Frederick Engels, provides a factual, scientific basis for a revolutionary perspective and for revolutionary optimism that dead-end capitalism can be uprooted and replaced by a rational and humane system based on human needs and desires, i.e., socialism.

The previously cited observation by Marx and Engels in *The Communist Manifesto* — that "the ruling ideas of each age have ever been the ideas of its ruling class" — motivated our exposure, in the first chapter of this book, of the intellectual absurdity of noted 20th century anthropologist Bronislaw Malinowski's position on the institution of marriage. We do not think professor Malinowski was an uninformed person. Far from it. What he was, however, was a praised and rewarded intellectual servitor for an imperialist ruling class that was, in the period of powerful and growing national liberation struggles in the first half of the 20th century, losing its hold on its colonial possessions and panicked by the growing strength and influence of the Soviet Union. Such epochal defeats tend to give rise to the most reactionary (and foolish) ideas. Malinowski, despite his erudition and lifetime of anthropological field-

Lolita Lebrón, Puerto Rican independentista.

work, was guilty of promulgating nonsense on the subject of pre-class "marriage" relations.

A scientific assessment of the evolution of human social/sexual relations is unacceptable to the rulers because it brings to the consciousness of the ruled not only the revelation that change is possible (actually, inevitable!), but also that it is the very essence of the material world and, thus, of human society. And this understanding, in turn, inspires confidence among the masses of exploited and oppressed working people that their struggles in support of social and economic justice and equality will eventually bear fruit.

Much of the first 15 chapters of this book focused on pre-class human societies. The overriding mes-

Freedom fighter and Civil War general Harriet Tubman

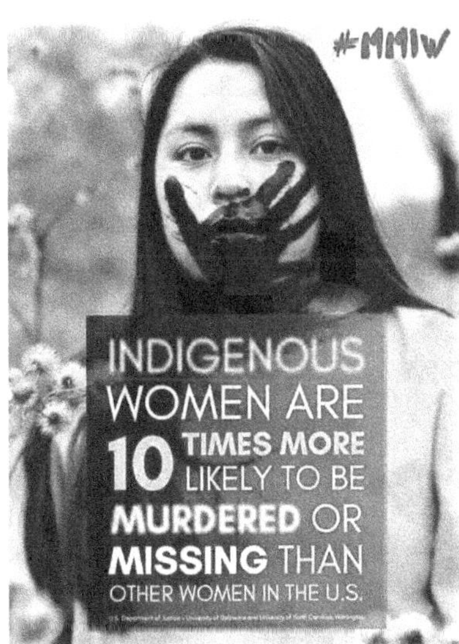

Leila Khaled, Palestinan liberation fighter

sage of this calculated emphasis on prehistory is that there is nothing natural or immutable about the subordinate social position that women have occupied through recorded history and up to the present day. Quite the contrary. The material we have reviewed has shown that the role of women in the evolution of our species has been pivotal.

That was the perspective of communist leader Dorothy Ballan:

> There is a virtual revolution going on in the minds of women. It is a harbinger of the general socialist revolution and at the same time is an indispensable ingredient for its success. (57)

Rani Velu Nachiyar of India fought British colonialism from 1780 to 1790.

Titina Silla, Guinea Bissau liberation fighter

Black Panther women

CHAPTER 39

The human capacity for love

lthough the main focus of this book has been on human social/sexual relations, there's been little mention of love. On the contrary, as has been noted over and over again, with the appearance of private property and the consequent introduction of economic inequality millennia ago, economic motives became the dominant force in the institution of marriage.

In Chapter 22, we noted Frederick Engels' observation in *Origin*:

> That the mutual affection of the people concerned should be the one paramount reason for marriage, outweighing everything else, was and always had been absolutely unheard of in the practice of the ruling classes; that sort of thing only happened in romance — or among the oppressed classes, who did not count. (142)

A little further along in that section of **Origin**, Engels writes:

> Full freedom of marriage can … only be generally established when the abolition of capitalist production and of the property relations created by it has removed all the accompanying economic considerations which still exert such a powerful influence on the choice of a marriage partner. For then there is no other motive left except mutual inclination. (144)

Still further along, he elaborates:

> What will quite certainly disappear from monogamy are
> all the features stamped upon it through its origin in
> property relations; these are, in the first place, supremacy
> of the man and secondly, the indissolubility of marriage.
> The supremacy of man in marriage is the simple conse-
> quence of his economic supremacy, and with the abolition
> of the latter will disappear of itself. The indissolubility of
> marriage is partly a consequence of the economic situation
> in which monogamy arose, partly tradition from the period
> when the connection between this economic situation and
> monogamy was not yet fully understood and was carried to
> extremes under a religious form.
>
> Today it is already broken through at a thousand points.
> If only the marriage based on love is moral, then also only
> the marriage is moral in which love continues. But the
> intense emotion of individual sex love varies very much in
> duration from one individual to another, especially among
> men, and if affection definitely comes to an end or is
> supplanted by a new passionate love, separation is a benefit
> for both partners as well as for society — only people will
> then be spared having to wade through the useless mire of
> a divorce case. (145)

In *Feminism and Marxism*, Dorothy Ballan raises the issue of sexual love as she analyzes the social significance of
the important technological breakthrough represented by
the development of the contraceptive pill:

> Like many previous inventions and discoveries, [the Pill]
> has brought about a virtual revolution in the social
> relations of many women, particularly as it affects the
> younger generation. ...
>
> The significant fact is that its simplicity of use has
> enabled the woman to control to a large degree her procre-
> ative function, and with little or no effort or discomfort.

It is in fact, for her, a technically revolutionary development in her centuries-old struggle to achieve release from the slavery imposed upon her by her inability to control this vital body function. …

For women, the accessibility of the Pill is in the nature of winning a civil right in the struggle for the rights of women. It obviously does not end oppression and discrimination against women, nor does it put an end to the ideology of male supremacy, but it helps clear some of the ground for the further development of the struggle. …

Promiscuity for men has existed as part and parcel of the monogamous family since its inception and has never been considered as affecting the so-called sanctity of the bourgeois family to any substantial degree. What enrages the bourgeoisie about "free love" is nothing more than the ability of women to participate in sex, and like men, without fear of pregnancy. (20-22)

The revolutionary task is to set love free

Ballan continues:

On the question of love, Marxists seek to focus not on "free love" but on how to set love free, that is, to emancipate love from the outmoded, artificial, social restraints which are the heritage of social systems based on class domination and class oppression. …

Love, which implies full freedom in human relations — whether with a marriage contract or not — cannot be the result of a mere relaxation of sex relations. Sex relations will always remain distorted as long as class oppression throttles human relations in general and relations between the sexes in particular. (22)

What has developed on an almost global basis since these words were written is widespread social awareness of the prevalence of sexual love between women, between men and between differently gendered people. In the U.S., the struggle for the right of same-sex couples to marry assumed the form of a mass, grassroots movement of lesbian, gay, bisexual, transgender, queer and two spirit people, with many allies among the heterosexual population.

Love as the basis of human solidarity

Among the nonsexual expressions of human love, unarguably the most important is the love that adults feel for children. Fidel Castro was once challenged by an arrogant bourgeois journalist about the supposed existence of specially privileged people within revolutionary Cuban society. Fidel's response was immediate and constituted an ideological body blow to the dumbfounded representative of U.S. imperialism: "Yes, we have a specially privileged group here. Our children!"

Decadent, late-stage capitalism is incapable of even approximating the situation in socialist Cuba, where the needs of children are the number one priority, where every child has a safe and secure home, is cared for, loved and offered every opportunity for personal growth and development.

Any Marxist commentary on love as a basic human emotion would be incomplete without a mention of its role in the context of the global struggle for a more just and humane world. What is the profound human solidarity shown by socialist and communist revolutionaries if not a supreme expression of the human capacity for feeling and expressing love?

In the book *Fidel and Religion: Fidel Castro in Conversation with Frei Betto on Marxism and Liberation Theology*, Brazilian liberation theologist Betto asks:

"Comandante, is love a revolutionary requirement?"

Castro replies:

If we go back to the first great social revolution — not the first socialist revolution, but the first great social revolution in the last few centuries: the French revolution — it had a three-word slogan: liberty, equality, fraternity. Liberty … was interpreted in a restricted way. It meant liberty for the bourgeoisie, for the whites; it didn't mean liberty for the African slaves. After they'd spread their ideas throughout the world, the French revolutionaries even sent armies to Haiti to crush the rebellion of the slaves who wanted liberty. After the independence of the United States, which had taken place before that, the slavery of Africans continued, as did the extermination of the Native Americans and all the other atrocities.

Therefore, the French revolution confined itself to liberty for the bourgeoisie and whites, and there was no equality at all, no matter how much philosophizing or talk there was about alleged equality in a society that was divided into classes. … I believe that only now, with socialism, can the concept of true liberty — full liberty — equality, and fraternity exist. I think that the precept of loving thy neighbor, of which the church speaks, is very concretely applied and implemented in the human equality, fraternity and solidarity upheld by socialism and in the internationalist spirit.

I believe that the fact that Cubans go to work in other lands as teachers, doctors, engineers, technicians and skilled workers and that tens of thousands — hundreds of thousands — are ready to do this under the most difficult conditions and at times at the cost of their lives, thus showing a supreme spirit of solidarity in loyalty to their principles, expresses the practical application of their respect, consideration and love for their fellow human beings. (Castro and Betto 2006: 256-257)

Mae Mallory and daughter Patricia,
bottom left. Mallory was prosecuted because she was a serious
proponent of armed self-defense against the fascist KKK.

CHAPTER 40

Final thoughts

The present effort has sought to support Frederick Engels' view of the social evolution of humanity with material evidence uncovered subsequent to the publication of **Origin of the Family, Private Property and the State** in 1884 and, specifically, to shed a historical materialist spotlight on the changing social position of women, LGBTQ2S people and the human social/sexual relationship usually referred to as marriage. We desire to stimulate the interest of the new generations of young social activists in the Marxist method, which includes not only a scientific analysis of past human social evolution but also an activist guide to a future free of oppression and exploitation through class struggle.

As they do with so many other social phenomena of importance to humanity, most bourgeois intellectuals and apologists for imperialism doggedly avoid subjecting the patterns and institutions of social/sexual relations to historical analysis. In so doing, in their role as servitors of the dominant class, they shamelessly deprive the workers and oppressed of an essential insight for their liberation: knowledge of the impermanence and transformation of all social phenomena.

In the course of the present effort, reference has been made to and quotations have been extracted from quite a large number of distinct sources. Basic bibliographic information has been provided for those readers so inclined to pursue further the subjects treated in these materials.

Most importantly, since this effort rests both ideologically and substantively on the writings of Karl Marx and Frederick Engels and, in particular, on Engels' *Origin*, it hopefully need not be stressed that the work of these pioneering communist revolutionaries continues — a century and a half later — to constitute supremely relevant guides to human thought and struggle in the present epoch of dead-end capitalism.

More specifically, the authoritative message to women in the pages of *Origin* is that for the many millennia of human existence before the rise of class-based oppression, women were free and equal partners with men, and the potential to regain that freedom and equality in all its beneficence for our species will coincide with the global overthrow of capitalism and a return to communalism and production for human use over production for private profit.

And also of critical importance, the presence in the human family of sex and gender variation, the added richness to our species that stems from the contributions of lesbian, gay, bisexual, transgender, queer and two spirit people, can no longer be ignored or denied. Their struggles globally in the last half century have made that clear. Knowledge of their socially beneficial roles in pre-class societies, their subsequent persecution and oppression with the onset of patriarchal class society, and their present struggle for full liberation is integral to a science-based understanding of human social evolution and the road to human liberation.

We Marxist revolutionaries are united in our belief that the destructive contradictions imposed on human society, including those that have distorted social/sexual relations ever since the imposition of private property, can only be resolved by capitalism's elimination.

The struggle continues!

In lieu of a Postscript: A homework assignment

Lifelong Marxist-Leninist Fred Goldstein, in the preface to his recent book, *Capitalism at a Dead End*, offers a timely homework assignment for readers of this book who are also activists in the struggles against racism and national oppression, sexual and gender oppression, and economic exploitation:

> There needs to be a serious conversation within the movement about what to replace the present system with. It is the thesis of this work that capitalism has reached a dead end. It is bringing humanity and the environment down. It must be abolished. The starting point for that conversation should be that the new society must be free of class exploitation; must be free of national, sexual and gender oppression; must put an end to war; must be free from all forms of domination and have respect for the planet. Above all, it must use the wealth of society to benefit all of society. (vii)

Las Soldaderas

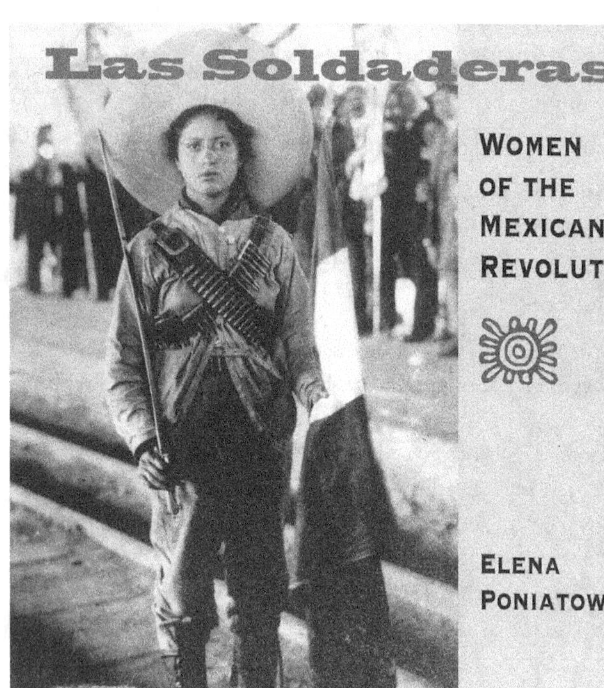

WOMEN
OF THE
MEXICAN
REVOLUTION

ELENA
PONIATOWSKA

Bibliography

Allen, N.J., H. Callan, R. Dunbar and W. James, eds. 2008. *Early Human Kinship: from Sex to Social Reproduction*. Oxford, England: Blackwell.

Bachofen, Johann Jakob. 2003-2008. *Mother Right*. Lewiston, N.Y.: Edwin Mellen.

Ballan, Dorothy. 1971. *Feminism and Marxism*. New York: World View Publishers.

Ballan, Dorothy. 1990. "When Goddesses Ruled: The Language of the Goddess Confirms Early Matriarchy." In *Liberation and Marxism*, June/July.

Benedict, Ruth. 1959. *Patterns of Culture*. New York: New American Library.

Besnier, Niko. 1996. "Polynesian Gender Liminality Through Time and Space." In *Third Sex, Third Gender: Beyond Sexual Dimorphism in Culture and History*. Gilbert Herdt, ed. New York: ZoneBooks, pp. 285-328.

Boué, Teresa Amarelle. 2019. "Statement by Teresa Amarelle Boué, Secretary General of FMC and Member of the Council of the State of the Republic of Cuba to the 63rd Session of the Commission on the Status of Women (CSW). New York, March 14, 2019." misiones.minrex.gob.cu.

Boyd, Robert and Joan Silk. 2012. *How Humans Evolved*. 6th ed. New York: Norton.

Briffault, Robert. 1956. *Marriage, Past and Present: A Debate Between Robert Briffault and Bronislaw Malinowski*. Boston: Porter Sargent.

Castro, Fidel. 1981. "The Revolution within the Revolution." In *Women and the Cuban Revolution*. Elizabeth Stone, ed. New York: Pathfinder Press, pp. 64-72.

Castro, Fidel. 2007. "History Will Absolve Me." In *The Fidel Castro Reader*. David Deutschmann and Deborah Shnookal, eds. Melbourne, Australia: Ocean Press.

Castro, Fidel and Frei Betto. 2006. *Fidel and Religion: Fidel Castro in Conversation with Frei Betto on Marxism and Liberation Theology*. Melbourne, Australia: Ocean Press.

Castro, Mariela. 2013. An interview with the French news agency AFP, reprinted online by elnuevoherald.com, Aug. 16.

Center for Cuban Studies. [no date] *Cuban Family Code.* "This translation of the Cuban Family Code ... is the official Cuban translation."

Cohen, Jon. 2010. *Almost Chimpanzee.* New York: St. Martin's Griffin.

Coontz, Stephanie. 2006. *Marriage, a History.* New York: Penguin Books.

Dahlberg, Frances, ed. *Woman the Gatherer.* 1981. New Haven: Yale University Press.

de Waal, Frans. 2005. *Our Inner Ape.* New York: Riverhead Books.

Deutschmann, David and Deborah Shnookal, eds. 2007. *The Fidel Castro Reader.* Melbourne, Australia: Ocean Press.

Dietler, Michael. 2001. "Theorizing the Feast: Rituals of Consumption, Commensal Politics, and Power in African Contexts." In *Feasts: Archaeological Perspectives on Food, Politics, and Power.* Michael Dietler and Brian Hayden, eds. Tuscaloosa, Ala.: University of Alabama Press, pp. 65-114.

Dietler, Michael and Brian Hayden, eds. 2001. *Feasts: Archaeological and Ethnographic Perspectives on Food, Politics, and Power.* Tuscaloosa, Ala.: University of Alabama Press.

Dietler, Michael and Ingrid Herbich. 2001. "Feasts and Labor Mobilization." In Michael Dietler and Brian Hayden, eds. 2001. *Feasts: Archaeological Perspectives on Food, Politics, and Power.* Tuscaloosa, Ala.: University of Alabama Press, pp. 240-264.

Drucker, Peter, ed. 2000. *Different Rainbows.* London: Millivres Ltd.

Dunbar, Robin. 2004. *The Human Story: A New History of Mankind's Evolution.* London: Faber and Faber.

Dunbar, Robin, Chris Knight and Camilla Power, eds. 1999. *The Evolution of Culture.* New Brunswick, N.J.: Rutgers University Press.

Engels, Frederick. 1935a. *Socialism: Utopian and Scientific.* New York: International Publishers.

Engels, Frederick. 1935b. "The Mark." In Frederick Engels. 1935a. *Socialism: Utopian and Scientific.* New York: International Publishers, pp. 77-93.

Engels, Frederick. 1950. *The Part Played by Labor in the Transition from Ape to Man.* New York: International Publishers.

Engels, Frederick. 1966. *The Peasant War in Germany.* New York: International Publishers.

Engels, Frederick. 1972. *The Origin of the Family, Private Property and the State.* New York: International Publishers.

Evans, Arthur. 1978. *Witchcraft and the Gay Counterculture*. Boston: Fag Rag Books.

Federici, Silvia. 2004. *Caliban and the Witch: Women, the Body and Primitive Accumulation*. Brooklyn, N.Y.: Autonomedia.

Feinberg, Leslie. 1992. *Transgender Liberation*. New York: World View Forum.

Feinberg, Leslie. 1993. *Stone Butch Blues*. Ithaca, N.Y.: Firebrand Books.

Feinberg, Leslie. 1996. *Transgender Warriors*. Boston: Beacon Press.

Feinberg, Leslie. 1998. *Trans Liberation*. Boston: Beacon Press.

Feinberg, Leslie. 2006. *Drag King Dreams*. New York: Carroll & Graf Publishers.

Feinberg, Leslie. 2009. *Rainbow Solidarity in Defense of Cuba*. New York: World View Forum.

Feinberg, Leslie. 2016. *Lavender & Red*. www.workers.org/books2016/Lavender_and_Red.pdf

Gailey, Christine Ward. 1987. *Kinship to Kingship*. Austin: University of Texas Press.

Gammage, Bill. 2011. *The Biggest Estate on Earth: How Aboriginal People Made Australia*. Sydney, Australia: Allen & Unwin.

Gimbutas, Marija. 1989. *The Language of the Goddess*. San Francisco: Harper and Row.

Goldstein, Fred. 2012. *Capitalism at a Dead End*. New York: World View Forum.

Goodall, Jane. 1986. *The Chimpanzees of Gombe: Patterns of Behavior*. Cambridge, Mass.: Harvard University Press.

Goodison, Lucy and Christine Morris, eds. 1999. *Ancient Goddesses: The Myths and the Evidence*. Madison, Wis.: University of Wisconsin Press.

Greenberg, David. 1988. *The Construction of Homosexuality*. Chicago: University of Chicago Press.

Gutiérrez, Ramón. 1991. *When Jesus Came, the Corn Mothers Went Away: Marriage, Sexuality, and Power in New Mexico, 1500-1846*. Stanford, Calif.: Stanford University Press.

Hager, Lori D., ed. 1997. *Women in Human Evolution*. London: Routledge.

Harris, Colette. 1995. "Socialist Societies and the Emancipation of Women: The Case of Cuba." In *Socialism and Democracy* 9:1, pp. 91-113.

Herdt, Gilbert, ed. 1996. *Third Sex, Third Gender: Beyond Sexual Dimorphism in Culture and History*. New York: ZoneBooks.

Herlihy, David. 1995. *Women, Family and Society in Medieval Europe.* Providence, R.I.: Berghahn Books.

Hodder, Ian. 2006. *The Leopard's Tale.* London: Thames and Hudson Ltd.

James, C.L.R. 1938. *The Black Jacobins.* London: Secker & Warburg.

Jacobs, Sue-Ellen, Wesley Thomas and Sabine Lang, eds. 1997. *Two-Spirit People: Native American Gender Identity, Sexuality, and Spirituality.* Urbana and Chicago: University of Illinois Press.

Katz, Jonathan. 1976. *Gay American History.* New York: Crowell.

Keeley, Lawrence. 1996. *War Before Civilization.* New York: Oxford University Press.

Klein, Richard. 2009. "Hominin Dispersals in the Old World." In *The Human Past.* Chris Scarre, ed. New York: Thames and Hudson, pp. 84-123.

Knight, Chris. 1991. *Blood Relations.* New Haven: Yale University Press.

Knight, Chris. 2008. "Early Human Kinship Was Matrilineal." In *Early Human Kinship.* N.J. Allen, H. Callan, R. Dunbar and W. James, eds. Oxford: Blackwell, pp. 61-82.

Kollontai, Alexandra. 1918. "V.I. Lenin and the First Congress of Women Workers." marxists.org/archive/kollonta/1918/congress.htm.

Leacock, Eleanor. 1981. *Myths of Male Dominance: Collected Articles on Women Cross-Culturally.* Chicago: Haymarket Books.

Leacock, Eleanor, Helen I. Safa and contributors. 1986. *Women's Work.* South Hadley, Mass.: Bergin and Garvey Publishers.

Leakey, Richard. 1994. *The Origin of Humankind.* New York: Basic Books.

Lee, Richard. 1968. "What Hunters Do for a Living." In *Man the Hunter.* Richard Lee and Irven DeVore, eds. New York: Aldine de Gruyter, pp. 30-48.

Lee, Richard and Irven Devore, eds. 1968. *Man the Hunter.* New York: Aldine de Gruyter.

Lenin, V.I. 1965. *The State and Revolution.* Peking: Foreign Languages Press.

Lenin, V.I. 1966. *The Emancipation of Women; from the writings of V.I. Lenin.* New York: International Publishers.

Lerner, Gerda. 1986. *The Creation of Patriarchy.* New York: Oxford University Press.

LeVay, Simon. 1996. *Queer Science.* Cambridge, Mass.: The MIT Press.

Lowie, Robert. 1920. *Primitive Society.* New York: Harper.

Martin, M. Kay and Barbara Voorhies. 1975. *Female of the Species.* New York: Columbia University Press.

Marx, Karl. 1906. *Capital: A Critique of Political Economy.* New York: The Modern Library.

Marx, Karl. 1965. *Pre-Capitalist Economic Formations.* New York: International Publishers.

Marx, Karl. 1969. *Genesis of Capital.* Moscow: Progress Publishers.

Marx, Karl. 1988. *Economic and Philosophical Manuscripts of 1844.* Amherst, N.Y.: Prometheus Books.

Marx, Karl and Frederick Engels. 1965. *Manifesto of the Communist Party.* Peking: Foreign Languages Press.

Marx, Karl and Frederick Engels. 1970. *The German Ideology.* New York: International Publishers.

Mauss, Marcel. 1990. *The Gift: The Form and Reason for Exchange in Archaic Societies.* Tr. by W.D. Halls. New York: Norton.

Mburu, John. 2000. "Awakenings: Dreams and Delusions of an Incipient Lesbian and Gay Movement in Kenya." In *Different Rainbows.* Peter Drucker, ed. London: Millivres Ltd., pp. 179-191.

McCubbin, Bob. 1993. *The Roots of Lesbian and Gay Oppression.* New York: WW Publishers.

Morgan, Lewis Henry. 1985. *Ancient Society.* Tucson: University of Arizona Press.

Morgan, Lewis Henry. 1996. *League of the Iroquois.* Secaucus, N.J.: Carol Publishing Group.

Morgan, Lewis Henry. 1997. *Systems of Consanguinity and Affinity of the Human Family.* Lincoln, University of Nebraska Press, reprinted from the original 1871 edition.

Mowat, Farley. 2005. *People of the Deer.* New York: Carroll & Graf Publishers.

Murray, Stephen and Will Roscoe, eds. 1998. *Boy-Wives and Female Husbands: Studies in African Homosexualities.* New York: Palgrave.

Neill, James. 2009. *The Origins and Role of Same-Sex Relations in Human Societies.* Jefferson, N.C., and London: McFarland and Company Inc.

Patterson, Orlando. 1985. *Slavery and Social Death: A Comparative Study.* Cambridge, Mass.: Harvard University Press.

Peterson, Jane. 2002. *Sexual Revolutions: Gender and Labor at the Dawn of Agriculture.* Walnut Creek: Altamira Press.

Reed, Evelyn. 1975. *Woman's Evolution.* New York: Pathfinder Press.

Reed, John. 1919. *Ten Days That Shook the World.* New York: International Publishers.

Reiter, Rayna, ed. 1975. *Toward an Anthropology of Women*. New York: Monthly Review Press.

Renfrew, Colin. 2007. *Prehistory: The Making of the Human Mind*. New York: Modern Library.

Roberts, J.M. 2004. *The New Penguin History of the World*. London: Penguin Books.

Roscoe, Will, ed. 1988. *Living the Spirit: A Gay American Indian Anthology*. New York: St. Martin's Press.

Ryan, Christopher and Cacilda Jethá. 2010. *Sex at Dawn*. New York: HarperCollins Publishers.

Sahlins, Marshall. 1972. *Stone Age Economics*. New York: Aldine de Gruyter.

Scarre, Chris, ed. 2009. *The Human Past*. 2nd ed. New York: Thames and Hudson.

Schneider, David and Kathleen Gough, eds. 1961. *Matrilineal Kinship*. Berkeley and Los Angeles: University of California Press.

Stone, Elizabeth, ed. 1981. *Women and the Cuban Revolution*. New York: Pathfinder Press.

Sun, Midnight. 1988. "Sex/Gender Systems in Native North America." In *Living the Spirit: A Gay American Indian Anthology*. Will Roscoe, ed. New York: St. Martin's Press, pp. 32-47.

Thwaites, Reuben Gold, ed. 1899. *The Jesuit Relations and Allied Documents*. Cleveland: Burrows Brothers Company.

Tiahui, M. 2019. "Celebrating Two-Spirit Pride – For thousands of years." *Struggle-La Lucha*, vol. 2, no. 11, June 1, p. 2.

Travis-Henikoff, Carole. 2008. *Dinner with a Cannibal*. Santa Monica: Santa Monica Press.

Trigger, Bruce. 2003. *Understanding Early Civilizations*. New York: Cambridge University Press.

Trotsky, Leon. 1973. *Problems of Everyday Life; and other writings on culture and science*. New York: Monad Press.

Trotsky, Leon. 1990. *In Defense of Marxism; the social and political contradictions of the Soviet Union*. New York: Pathfinder Press.

Turke, Paul. 1984. "Effects of ovulatory concealment and synchrony on protohominid mating systems and parental roles." In *Ethology and Sociobiology* 5, pp. 33-44.

Wagner, Sally Roesch. 2001. *Sisters in Spirit: Haudenosaunee (Iroquois) Influence on Early American Feminists*. Summertown, Tenn.: Native Voices.

Williams, Walter. 1988. *The Spirit and the Flesh*. Boston: Beacon Press.

Wrangham, Richard and Dale Peterson. 1996. *Demonic Males*. Boston: Houghton Mifflin.

Index

www.ingramcontent.com/pod-product-compliance
Lightning Source LLC
Chambersburg PA
CBHW061334250726
48657CB00004B/1153